1098 / 135
AUT

£2.50

5998

Saints and Symbols

Altarpiece —
The Virgin and Child with Saints Catherine of Alexandria and Siena by Ambrogio Bergognone

AN ILLUSTRATED
HISTORY OF  Saints
and
Symbols

OLWEN REED

SPURBOOKS LIMITED

Published by Spurbooks Limited
6 Parade Court, Bourne End,
Buckinghamshire

ISBN 0 904978 31 1

Designed and produced by
Mechanick Exercises, London

Typesetting by Inforum, Portsmouth
Printed in Great Britain by
Tonbridge Printers Limited
Peach Hall Works, Tonbridge, Kent

Contents

Illustrations

CHAPTER 1

The Making of a Saint

What exactly is a saint? In everyday life we come across saints' names so frequently, applied to buildings, streets and towns, that we no longer associate them with real people. Sometimes the name of a church, like St Paul's in London, St Mark's in Venice, St Peter's in Rome, or even our own parish church, may make us think briefly of the person behind the name, but to most of us St Andrew's conjures up pictures of golf rather than thoughts about the first disciple, and a Catherine-wheel is a firework rather than the martyrdom instrument of the young saint of Alexandria. Many towns, from San Francisco, Sao Paolo and Santiago, to our own St Helen's, St Alban's and St Leonard's-on-Sea, are obviously named after saints, but who ever gives their eponyms a thought? The list is endless: the St Lawrence River, le Mont St Michel, St. Bartholomew's Hospital, St Pancras station, St Bernard dogs, the plant St John's Wort, the illness St Vitus' dance, Valentine cards, and so on. Once you start looking for such names, they strike you in newspaper items, road signs and even on goods in the shopping basket.

Ireland, Wales, Cornwall and Brittany are particularly rich in saintly names because of the activities of the Celtic missionary saints of the 6th and 7th centuries. They travelled far afield and legend has embroidered their adventures; some are credited with having crossed the sea on a mill-stone, a cloak, or even a leaf. Cornwall has a large share of the country's ancient chapels and holy wells, and half the villages seem to be named after one saint or another. The Welsh prefix

St Michael defeating dragon and weighing souls of the dead

'Llan' which now means 'church', was originally applied to the enclosure around a religious settlement, and it is frequently followed by the name of a saint. Llanfair, the church of St Mary, is a popular combination.

So, what is a saint? In Old Testament times the term applied to all Israelites, as God's 'chosen people'. In the New Testament it meant anyone belonging to a Christian community. It did not necessarily imply any special holiness, but the Resurrection was then a sufficiently recent event for Christians to cling passionately to their faith and be ready to die for it.

The majority of Christian martyrs belong to the period when Rome dominated the Western world. The Romans had their own gods who distributed lavish favours or feasome punishments to those who displeased them. There were also household gods, the '*lares*' and '*penates*', and the occasional Emperor who was declared divine. In addition, a number of gods were taken over from conquered tribes or the Egyptians, so they would in all probability have been quite willing to turn a blind eye to yet another one, the Christian God.

The Christians, however, would not accept the idea of their God being one among so many. The basic tenet of their belief was that there was only one true God and all others were false. They refused to acknowledge the divinity of the Emperor, and so were accused of treason. This brave defiance led to appalling persecution, but the martyrs showed such outstanding courage that each new death inspired more converts. Their graves were turned into altars, each a focal point where Christians gathered to honour the martyr who had perished there. Such an emotionally charged atmosphere was right for the occurrence of miracles, and later on hopeful pilgrims came to pray at the shrines. Sometimes the relics were removed to another resting place of more distinction; frequently they were stolen, and over the centuries they were often divided so that several churches claimed to have a few sacred bones from one particular saint.

In the beginning the veneration accorded to a martyr was always spontaneous. He or she became a saint by 'acclamation'. If the local bishop was satisfied that the martyr was worthy of veneration, he gave his official approval. Each year, on the anniversary of the saint's death, local people came to the tomb to honour the memory, and gradually the fame of the particular saint spread, bringing pilgrims from ever further afield.

The question of martyrdom presented several problems. Should it include those who had no choice in the matter, or only those who could have saved themselves by recanting but refused to do so? Should it include those who deliberately sought martyrdom, like the Donatists of North Africa, who, in the 4th century were so convinced that martyrdom was the only route to salvation that they threatened to kill anyone who refused to help them on their way! In the 16th century there was the problem of those put to death by their fellow Christians, Catholics by Protestants and vice-versa, all equally convinced that they were carrying out God's will. Finally, there is a whole host of Eastern saints unrecognised by the Western Church.

The word 'martyr' originally meant simply 'one who bears witness'. For the first three hundred years, bearing witness to the Christian faith almost invariably led to a violent death, so the term acquired its more limited meaning. After the Emperor Constantine's conversion in 313 AD, there were fewer martyrs, and the qualification for sainthood became a noble life rather than a noble death. Saints in this category are known as confessors. Like 'martyr', the word 'confessor' meant witness, but the two words developed along different lines. A number of confessor saints were hermits. At first it was a case of escaping from persecution, and many settled in caves around the Red Sea. Later, however, a man might deliberately choose to withdraw from family and friends and live alone, leaving society, with the highest possible motives, seeking nothing from anyone and devoting himself entirely to God, even mortifying the flesh to concentrate on spiritual matters. He usually found a cave for shelter, with a nearby spring of fresh water, and lived off the land unless neighbouring villagers discovered his whereabouts and brought food. Sometimes others joined him, and eventually a monastery might be founded.

Villagers were proud of their hermits, and no doubt frequently exaggerated the tales of any miracle performed. The power of healing was ascribed not only to a saint's relics, but also to the waters of his holy well. A local saint therefore, was quite an asset, and no chance of acquiring one was missed. When approval was left to the bishops, the number of saints increased so rapidly that by the 12th century the whole thing had got out of hand, and the Pope decided to intervene.

In 933, Pope John XV had canonised St Ulrich, Bishop of Augsburg, but the bishops still retained the right until Alexander III (1159-1181) insisted that the Pope's assent must be given before anyone could be declared a saint, and in 1234 Gregory IX made this a law.

The rather haphazard requirements for sainthood were defined in 1199 by Pope Innocent III. He laid down two basic rules: the prospective saint must have led a life of heroic virtue, and also be proved to have performed miracles *after his death*. Miracles performed during his life-time were not enough as it was presumed that these could have been managed with the aid of the devil.

Nowadays the process is deliberately slow and complicated, involving three stages : Veneration, Beatification, and Canonisation. Any member of the Roman Catholic Church who has good cause for doing so, can put forward a name to the Bishop. In the 'Ordinary Processes' the 'postulator' begins collecting and sifting evidence, while the 'Devil's Advocate' searches out all possible objections. If the would-be saint is deemed worthy of veneration, he passes on to the second stage, the 'Apostolic Processes', which involve several sittings of the Sacred Congregation and a painstakingly thorough examination of all the claims. There must be irrefutable evidence that the candidate has performed at least two miracles, (medical evidence is naturally taken into account) and has possessed to an outstanding degree the seven virtues: Faith, Hope, Charity, Prudence, Justice, Fortitude, and Temperance.

Most of us could claim to practise a few of these from time to time, but to keep to all of them all the time, one would need to be — well, a saint! Martyrs were occasionally excused some of these requirements, as their heroic death was considered sufficient proof of their worthiness. The Pope presides at the final phases of the investigation, and if all goes well he issues a decree of beatification.

Further investigation, with more sittings of the Sacred Congregation, leads to canonisation, but there must be proof of two further miracles having taken place *after* beatification. Then, on a duly appointed day, the solemn rite at St Peter's in Rome takes place. This is an intensely emotional and impressive ceremony. The whole process of canonisation is always carried out with meticulous care and can take hundreds of years.

Immediately after canonisation, the new saint's name is placed in the Calendar of Saints. He is allotted a feast day, his relics are given a place of honour, and in future he may be depicted in art, sculpture or stained glass, with a halo. Offerings to God may be made in his name and churches may be dedicated to him. He may be invoked in prayers, but his soul must no longer be prayed for as he is presumed to have progressed beyond such a need.

In recent years both Ireland and Scotland have acquired a new saint. Oliver Plunket, Primate of All Ireland in the reign of Charles II, was canonised on the 12th October 1975, the first official Irish saint since Lawrence O'Toole, Archbishop of Dublin in the reign of Henry II.

St Oliver Plunket was born of wealthy parents in County Meath in 1629. As frequently happened to younger sons at that time, he was sent to Rome to study for the priesthood. Scholarly and elegant, he thoroughly enjoyed his time there and was in no hurry to return to Ireland. However, in 1669 he was sent to replace the Archbishop of Armagh who had died in exile. After a long period of repression the Church of Ireland was sadly disorganised and he immediately set about restoring order. One of his minor but memorable reforms was to forbid the priests to drink whiskey. He worked himself into a state of exhaustion among the poor, and was greatly loved by them. In 1673, the repression of the Catholics worsened and Oliver Plunket was forced into hiding. English Protestants were already nervous and inclined to see Papists everywhere, when the Titus Oates plot brought things to a head. Unfortunately it was just at this time that the Archbishop was betrayed, arrested, and taken to London to undergo a mockery of a trial. On the 1st July 1681 he was hanged at Tyburn, disembowelled and quartered. St Oliver Plunket's head is preserved at Drogheda and most of his body at Downside Abbey near Bath, although parts of it

Tympanum, Autun — showing the weighing of souls

have been sent elsewhere, including bits to Armagh Cathedral. He was beatified in 1920 by Pope Benedict XV and canonised fifty-five years later.

St Margaret of Scotland, the wise and gentle wife of King Malcolm III, lived at the end of the 11th century and was canonised in 1249. There was then no new Scottish saint until the 17th October 1976, when John Ogilvie was canonised. He was born in Banffshire in 1579, and at the age of thirteen was sent abroad to study. He travelled all over the Continent and was converted to Catholicism, becoming a Jesuit priest while in Paris in 1610.

Catholics were being persecuted in Scotland, and John Ogilvie was anxious to return to help them. In 1610 he was allowed to go secretly, so on landing he pretended to be a discharged army officer trading in horses. For a year he travelled about in disguise and even managed to visit the Catholics held prisoner in Edinburgh Castle. In the autumn of 1614 he was betrayed in Glasgow and thrown in gaol. For five months he resisted all attempts to force him to acknowledge James I as the spiritual head instead of the Pope, but on the 10th March 1615 he was hanged in Glasgow. Eventually, in 1929, he was beatified by Pope Pius XI.

Several miraculous cures were ascribed to St John Ogilvie, but only one was considered irrefutable, and in this case Pope Paul ruled that one was enough. This important one concerned a Glasgow man who was apparently dying of stomach cancer until he and his wife prayed to Father Ogilvie. The couple were at the canonisation ceremony in St Paul's Basilica together with many members of the present Ogilvie family.

Lives of recent saints are fairly well documented, but when writing about earlier ones it is difficult to be strictly accurate. No two sources seem to agree on all the facts. This is a common problem when dealing with events which occurred before reliable written records were kept, and in the case of the saints it is also complicated by emotion. For centuries, stories of their lives were handed down by word of mouth, always an unreliable process, and no doubt a colourful imagination or wishful thinking altered the slant. When historical facts were short, legend filled in the gaps. Lives of the Celtic saints in particular, were man, Jacobus de Voragine, a 13th-century Archbishop of Genoa. He was so fascinated by hagiography that he searched out every available scrap of information and put it all together, both fact and fiction, in a book which he called *Legenda Aurea*, the Golden Legend. Although written in Latin it was widely read and translated. In those days legend simply meant something to be read (gerundive of '*Legere*' — to read). It was not necessarily fictional, but a good deal of the Golden Legend almost certainly was.

Some two hundred years later an English cloth merchant, William Caxton, settled in Bruges. He enjoyed reading and wanted to write but found the task of producing books by hand too slow and laborious, so in 1476 he returned to London and set up his first printing press in England at Westminster. Among the earliest books to be printed in English was his collection of stories from the Golden Legend, increasing the interest in the lives of the saints.

Since those early days, saints' days have been added to the calendar at a much slower rate and several have been deleted altogether. Both the Roman Catholic and Anglican Churches have pruned their lists; the Church of England has recently reduced the number of lesser Church festivals from two hundred to eighty. Unfortunately some of those to be dropped — considered to be the least authenticated — include some of the most popular ones. St Valentine's demotion is not surprising as his fame is largely due to the fact that his feast day coincides with a pagan festival, but St Catherine of Alexandria is a well-loved saint and has many churches dedicated to her. The elimination of St Nicholas, the patron saint of sailors and children will disappoint his followers, but his association with Christmas, as Santa Claus, is too strong to allow him to disappear altogether.

Why have saints at all? If we have complaints or feel we need help, why not go straight to the chief? There are many who would not know how to begin praying to God without the intercession of some saint who, they believe, favours them or can sympathise with their particular problem. A journalist once summed it up very neatly, by describing richly embroidered with fanciful stories, and accounts vary from country to country and from town to town.

Much of our knowledge of the early saints is due to the efforts of one the saints as a celestial box number for forwarding applications to the Almighty.

However we feel about the saints, it has to be admitted that they set a very encouraging example, showing that ordinary men and women can attain the greatest heights, and in a dangerous and often dreary world they bring a message of hope.

CHAPTER 2
Biblical Saints

In New Testament times, Palestine was part of the Roman Empire. Its three main divisions, Galilee in the North, Samaria in the middle, and Judaea in the South, had their own rulers, notably Herod who was King of Judaea at the time of Jesus' birth. They all owed allegiance, however, to the Roman Emperor. This allegiance was given grudgingly by many of the Jews who resented Roman influence, and there were dangerous under-currents of unrest. For many, the teachings of Jesus only complicated matters still further. Was this really their long-awaited Messiah or just another trouble-maker?

Although Jesus was born in Judaea, he spent most of his life in Galilee, first as a boy at Nazareth and then teaching and healing in the area around the inland sea. His first disciples were fishermen on the Sea of Galilee, and they made their headquarters at the lakeside town of Capernaum. Galilee can therefore claim a large share of the New Testament saints.

First in importance among the biblical saints is, of course, St Mary the Virgin, the epitome of purity and perfect womanhood, venerated by millions throughout the centuries. After the childhood of Jesus, Mary is mentioned in the Gospels only occasionally; at the wedding in Cana, for example, and most poignantly at the Crucifixion when Jesus entrusted her to John's care. Nothing certain is known about her later life, although it has been the subject of many writings and legends. She has, however, been an unfailing source of inspiration, not only from the religious point of view but also in art and literature.

The Nativity.

Robed in blue, the colour of purity, she has been portrayed in everything from paintings of the Old Masters to school nativity plays.

Strangely there is no mention in the Bible of her parents, but according to an apochryphal account they were a wealthy but childless couple called Ann and Joachim. Their childlessness was considered a matter for reproach and because of it the high priest refused to accept Joachim's generous offering at the temple. Joachim was so upset that he went off by himself for forty days and forty nights — a popular period in those days.

Towards the end of this time, Ann came across a nest of sparrows in a bush and the sight of the little fledglings increased her distress as it seemed to her that only she in all the world remained childless. While she wept an angel appeared and told her the wonderful news that she would have a child. She met Joachim by the Golden Gate of the temple, and together they vowed that they would give the promised child to God. Accordingly when the child, Mary, was three years old, they handed her over to the priests at the temple. One account states that they died shortly afterwards without seeing her again, but this view was not accepted by artists in succeeding centuries, for St Ann appears in many pictures and stained glass windows, and is often shown teaching her small daughter to read. There is a theory that Ann and Joachim had another daughter, Salome, who was the mother of the apostles James and John.

St Ann is a much-loved saint with countless churches dedicated to her. She is the patron saint of Brittany and (with St Joseph) of Canada. She is also the patron saint of housewives and pregnant women.

St Joseph was of the House of David, a carpenter of Nazareth and a 'just man'. That is all the direct information to be gleaned from the Gospels. It seems probable that Joseph died before Jesus began his ministry, and he must certainly have died before the Crucifixion, or he would have been there with Mary. Traditionally he is supposed to have been much older than Mary, perhaps a widower with children of his own already. James the Just, who later organised the Christian Church in Jerusalem, may well have been Jesus' half-brother.

Like Joachim and Ann, the priest Zacharias and his wife Elizabeth had also given up hope of having children. Their story and the events leading up to the birth of John the Baptist, are told in St Luke's Gospel. The baby had an auspicious start in life, for his mother was a cousin of Mary the Virgin. Mary and Elizabeth spent much time together while they were both awaiting the birth of their sons.

As a young man, John spent a considerable time in the wilderness, living on locusts and wild honey and dressed in camel skins, and perhaps it was this unusual garment which eventually made him the patron saint of tailors! John's teaching caused a tremendous stir and people flocked to be baptised by him in the River Jordan. Eventually John was imprisoned for daring to criticise Herod Antipas by speaking out against what he considered to be a sinful marriage between Herod and Herodias, former wife of Herod's half-brother, Philip. Her-

St Ann and St Joachim at the Golden Gate

odias naturally felt threatened and hoped for the death of John the Baptist. Her opportunity came at the King's birthday feast when the daughter of Herodias, Salome, danced so beautifully that Herod promised her anything she cared to ask for. Prompted by her mother, Salome asked for John's head. Herod reluctantly kept his promise and the prisoner's decapitated head was gorily brought to the banquet on a silver platter. The scene has provided a source of inspiration to artists ever since.

The feast days of most saints are celebrated on the anniversary of their death, which to them means entry into a new life. John the Baptist is an exception; his feast day, the 24th June, is the anniversary of his birth. As St John's Eve happened to coincide with Midsummer Eve, it was associated with the old pagan Midsummer festivals, particularly that of lighting bonfires.

Among John the Baptist's disciples was a Galilean fisherman named Andrew, who became so convinced by Jesus' teaching that he fetched his brother Simon Peter, saying with absolute certainty, 'We have found the Messiah'. Because of this Andrew is called *Protoclet* — 'first called', and St Bede refers to him as the 'Introducer'. This incident is recounted in the Gospel of St John, but other Gospel-writers describe how Jesus called two pairs of brothers, Andrew and Peter, and James and John. All four were fishermen on the Sea of Galilee. After these early incidents, Andrew is mentioned in the Bible on only a few occasions, but he seems to have been a friendly, approachable man, ready to listen to people and to act on what he heard. Although biblical references to Andrew are brief, he figures largely in apocryphal writings.

While we learn little from the Bible about Andrew's character, that of his brother Peter comes over very clearly, compelling our admiration for his good qualities of loyalty, faith, energy, courage and enthusiasm, but at the same time arousing our sympathy and understanding for his very human failings. Peter was rash and impetuous, blurting out tactless questions, was often over-confident of his own ability and made promises he could not keep. Peter's biggest failure was the denial of his association with Jesus, but when he realised what he had done, he wept bitterly, and the experience seems to have finally taught him the lesson of humility.

23

Peter was originally known as Simon, but this was changed by Jesus to Peter, meaning rock. Succeeding popes, of whom Peter became the first, have usually followed this practice of changing their names. Jesus said Peter was to be the rock on which the Church would be built, and so it came about. Peter was always the leader and spokesman of the disciples. With James and John he was present at all the-principal events and played a leading part.

Peter organised the selection of another apostle to replace the traitor Judas. He was also the first apostle to perform a miracle, by curing a crippled beggar by the Gate of the Temple after Pentecost. When the apostles began their missionary travels, Peter went first to Samaria with John. Then he settled in Rome and established the Church there, no mean feat for a humble Galilean fisherman, for Rome was then the sophisticated centre of world power as well as of vice and corruption. While James became head of the Church in Jerusalem, and Paul devoted his energies to converting the Gentiles, Peter concentrated on the Jews in Rome, arousing the bitter hatred of the priests. He was forbidden to preach and imprisoned and scourged for doing so. His release by an angel from his prison chains is commemorated in those churches dedicated to *St Peter ad Vincula*. In spite of great difficulties he succeeded in making Rome the world centre of Christianity, and became the first of an unbroken line of popes.

Peter is credited with two epistles, and although he did not write a Gospel, that of St Mark is based largely on Peter's teaching and the memory of first-hand experience. Mark acted as Peter's secretary and interpreter and this makes the second Gospel particularly interesting. Peter is generally supposed to have lived to a great age before being martyred in Rome under Nero. He was, at his own request, crucified upside down, because he felt he was unworthy of the same death as Jesus. He was buried at the spot where the high altar of the Vatican now stands. Peter is often described as the 'keeper of the pearly gates' because Jesus promised him the keys of Heaven, and he is frequently portrayed holding either one or two keys.

Of the twelve apostles, the three who were particularly close to Jesus, were Peter, James and John. James and John were the sons of Zebedee and Salome, and before following Jesus they had worked as fishermen. Jesus nicknamed them both *Boanerges*, Sons of Thunder. James was certainly hot-tempered and ambitious, and often had to be rebuked by Jesus.

After the martyrdom of Stephen, James (referred to as *The Great* to distinguish him from the other apostle of the same name) travelled westwards, possibly even as far as Spain. Whether or not he actually reached Spain, his relics were eventually taken there, and his shrine at Compostella became a tremendously important place of pilgrimage. He is the patron saint of Spain, and because the Conquistadores took his cult to the New World, he is also the patron saint of Chile, whose capital, Santiago, is named after him.

Although Stephen has the honour of being the first Christian martyr, James was the first of the apostles to die for his faith. He returned to Judaea in 43 AD and the following year was put to death with the sword by Herod Agrippa, grandson of Herod the Great. As often happened in such cases, his accuser was so impressed by his noble death that he was converted!

The Crossed Keys of St Peter

In the Acts of the Apostles we find Peter and John also working tremendously hard. In Samaria they confirmed thousands by the laying on of hands; they founded the Seven Churches of Asia Minor, and John became head of the Church in Asia. In the time of Domitian, John was exiled to the island of Patmos and later settled in Ephesus. One of the more colourful stories about him was later discredited; on Domitian's order he was supposedly boiled in oil but miraculously escaped unharmed. The church of *San Giovanni in Olio* in Rome commemorates the event. St John, called the Divine, or the Evangelist, is believed to have written the fourth Gospel, three epistles and the Book

25

of Revelation, a considerable output which accounts for his being the patron saint of writers, publishers and booksellers! When he was too old to preach, so St Jerome tells us, he kept repeating 'Little children, love one another'. His followers wanted a more eloquent sermon, but he told them, 'It is the Lord's command, and if this alone be done, it is enough.'

The twelve apostles worked together in pairs. The first three pairs were Andrew and Peter, James and John, Philip and Bartholomew. Philip was one of the first disciples to be called, and he in turn fetched his friend Nathaniel (Bartholomew). Of Philip the Apostle we know very little. He was the provisioner; one of his more daunting jobs was having to feed the five thousand, and so he is the patron saint of pastry-cooks. Of Philip the Deacon, who may well have been the same person, we know a good deal more.

While the twelve apostles were busy with this evangelical work, they appointed seven deacons to look after the welfare of the Christian communities. Philip, who was one of these, did the spadework in Samaria before Peter and John arrived to establish the Church there. Philip's main work was carried out in Central Asia where he proved to be an energetic administrator. He is believed to have died at Hierapolis, where the people worshipped a gigantic snake, or in some versions, a dragon. Philip and Bartholomew together made many converts, including Nicanora, the wife of the procunsul. Nicanora's husband was far from pleased and had the two apostles cruelly tortured. Bartholomew was hung up by his hair and Philip by his feet. Philip prayed for the earth to open and swallow the crowd who were witnessing their sufferings. The prayer was granted, but Jesus appeared and reproved him, making the sign of the Cross which turned into a ladder. The seven thousand heathen bystanders climbed up, repented and were saved, but the wicked Proconsul and the giant serpent were unable to use the holy ladder. A martyrdom colourfully embroidered by legend! Philip was punished for his unworthy prayer by being excluded from Paradise for forty days, and he asked Bartholomew and the new converts to pray for him. Where his blood had dripped a vine grew, complete with grapes, within three days. The people were told to use the wine from the grapes in their daily communion, and at the end of forty

26

days Philip appeared again and said he was now admitted to Paradise and all was well.

Philip's friend, called Nathaniel by St John, but Bartholomew by the other evangelists, travelled in partnership with him. Very few facts are known about Bartholomew, but the story-tellers have filled in the gaps. One fanciful tale relates how he cured a princess who had lost her reason and went around biting people! Her father was so delighted with the cure that he was ready to accept Bartholomew's teaching. For good measure the apostle called out the devil which had taken up residence in an idol. The statue fell to the ground in pieces and the devil, covered with spikes like a hedgehog and snorting fire like a dragon, scurried away. An angel appeared, seized the strange creature and carried it off. Unfortunately the King's brother, also a King, had been very fond of the statue and was so angry when it was smashed that he had Bartholomew beaten with clubs and then beheaded. However, a later and more widely accepted story says that Bartholomew was flayed alive. For this reason his symbol is a knife and he is usually portrayed holding one.

In Michelangelo's *Last Judgement* in the Sistine Chapel, he is shown dangling his flayed skin like a crumpled overcoat. Bartholomew's much travelled relics are now preserved in a church on St Bartholomew's Island in the Tiber. His gruesome death made him the patron saint of tradesmen associated with knives and hides, like butchers, tanners, glove-makers and furriers.

St Matthew, whose gospel was supposedly taken to India by St Bartholomew, shares with St John the distinction of being both one of the twelve apostles and one of the four apostles and evangelists. He lived at Capernaum, a busy little port on the north-western shore of the Sea of Galilee. It was the administrative centre of the area and a frontier town with a customs post. Matthew (also called Levi) was the only wealthy man among the twelve apostles. He was a publican, not in the modern sense of the word, but a tax-gatherer. They were extremely unpopular even in those days, and are often referred to in the Bible in the same breath as sinners. He was really the equivalent of a Customs and Excise Officer at Capernaum, and was on duty at his desk when he decided to follow Jesus. According to various sources, Matthew preached in Persia, Macedonia, and even Ethiopia, but there is no historical record of his travels nor of how he met his death. He is generally assumed to have died by the sword, but here again there is a more fanciful story. When he came to the gates of a pagan city, so the story goes, he stuck his staff into the ground. Immediately it grew into a tree covered with fruit, and a spring gushed at its foot. Inhabitants of the city who ate the fruit and bathed in the spring water realised at once that they had been worshipping false gods. Their rejection made the king extremely angry and he had Matthew first saturated with oil and then covered with burning pitch. The fire got out of hand and not only melted the gold and silver idols but threatened to consume the king himself. He cried to the dying apostle for help and the fire was extinguished. Matthew was buried far out at sea, but was seen ascending to Heaven accompanied by two angels. He prophesied, correctly, that within three years the pagan king would become a Christian bishop.

Like the other three evangelists, St Matthew has a winged symbol; his is an angel. His other attributes are money bags and the sword of his martyrdom. Because of his early career as a tax-gatherer, he is the patron saint of anyone connected with finance.

Matthew's working partner was Thomas, called 'Didymus'. Both his names mean 'twin', in Aramaic and Greek, but no mention is ever made of his twin brother or sister. St John's Gospel gives us a fair idea of Thomas' character, slow to accept new ideas, but brave and loyal. He showed courage and devotion but was not a man to whom absolute faith came easily. According to legend, St Thomas founded the Church in Southern India, settling at Mylapore, now a suburb of the city of Madras; the Christians of the area are still called St Thomas' Christians. In 53 AD Thomas was put to death on the King's orders, stabbed by a soldier with a spear. In the 16th century when Portuguese settlers excavated the site of the martyrdom on a hilltop near the town, bones and a spearhead were found and a chapel was erected on the spot. Later San Thome Cathedral was built on the site of the saint's supposed burial place. His relics were moved first to Edessa in Mesopotamia and later to Ortona in Italy. The symbol of St Thomas, a carpenter by trade, is a carpenter's rule.

James the Less, son of Alpheus, is distinguished by his title from

James the Great, brother of John and son of Zebedee. James the Less, a great administrator, became head of the Church in Jerusalem where there was such bitter opposition to the Christians that his martyrdom was inevitable. Eventually he was taken to the roof of the temple and, with a hostile crowd waiting below, ordered to deny Christ's teaching. When he refused he was thrown from the parapet and his broken body then beaten with a fuller's club by one of mob. For this reason he is represented in art holding a club. So, confusingly, is Thaddeus, better known as Jude.

The Sailing Vessel of St Jude

St Jude must hold the record for getting his name in the newspapers. Scarely a day goes by without one or other of the personal column announcements carrying a note of thanks to St Jude 'for favours received'. He is the patron saint of the desperate, and sadly a great many people feel the need to invoke him. Of the man himself we know almost nothing except that he was probably the brother of Simon and may, like him, have been a Zealot. They are believed to have worked together in Persia where they were both martyred, Jude being beaten to death and Simon sawn into pieces — hence Simon's symbol is a saw, and Jude is sometimes portrayed with the sailing vessel symbol representing the Church, which he took to many places during his missionary work. Jude is also known as St Thaddeus or St Lebbaeus.

The Zealots were a group of Jewish nationalists whose activities finally led to the destruction of Jerusalem by Titus in 70 AD and to the dispersal of the Jews. Simon was certainly a member and is often referred to in the Bible as 'Simon the Zealot' or 'the Cananaean' which meant the same thing.

After Pentecost, Peter had to organize the selection of a replacement for Judas Iscariot. It had to be someone with first-hand experience of Jesus' teaching, and of two possible candidates the one finally chosen was Matthias. Matthias was eventually beheaded at Colchis, and his symbol is an axe.

As the number of Christians increased, the apostles, finding that they were wasting precious evangelising time in administration, appointed seven deacons to deal with the more mundane problems. The first to be appointed was Stephen, a Hellenistic Jew, whose special task was to see that Greek-speaking Christian widows were treated fairly. The Hellenists were unpopular in Jerusalem, especially among the Jewish scribes. Stephen was an eloquent preacher who 'did great wonders and miracles among the people'. His success aroused jealousy and mistrust and he was summoned before the Sanhedrin, the high priest's court, to answer charges of blasphemy. Far from admitting any guilt, he lashed out at his judges with the full force of his oratory, calling them 'stiff-necked' and accusing them of killing Jesus. Not surprisingly he was condemned to death by stoning, and dragged outside the city walls for the sentence to be carried out. His death was watched approvingly by a fanatical young Jew called Saul, who was later to change sides in a highly dramatic fashion. Stephen was the first Christian martyr; his death took place around 35 AD, about nine years before that of James the Great, the first of the apostles to be martyred. Some four hundred years later a monk was told in a dream that Galamiel, St Paul's teacher, had buried Stephen's body in his garden. The relics were recovered and taken to Rome to share a shrine with those of St Lawrence. This was when St Lawrence is said to have earned his title of 'the Courteous Spaniard' by moving over in his sarcophagus so that the protomartyr could have the place of honour on the right-hand side.

From the first moment of their calling, the twelve apostle-saints spent all their time with Jesus, working with him, trying to follow his teaching, and endeavouring to understand him. They could have had little idea that in two thousand years' time people would still be won-

St Simon the Apostle

30

dering about Jesus, or surely they would have kept a detailed day-to-day record of his words and deeds. Instead, all four Gospels were written after the death of Jesus; how long after is the subject of much conjecture, but after careful analysis by a number of scholars, the main conclusion seems to be that only one of the Gospels, St Luke's, could have been written by the supposed author. The arguments are so complicated that many people adhere to the simple belief that the first Gospel was written primarily for the Jews by St Matthew, the ex-publican; the second by St Mark, whose information came from the personal recollections of St Peter; the third by St Luke, friend and physician of St Paul, and the last by St John, when he was a very old man looking back over his eventful life.

St Mark, the supposed author of the second Gospel, lived in Jerusalem. His mother Mary was a devout Christian, and her home was frequently used by the Christians as a meeting place. It was here that St Peter went after being freed by the angel from Herod's prison.

A cousin of St Mark, St Barnabas of Cyprus, was also a friend of St Paul. Barnabas and Paul took Mark with them on their initial missionary journey, first to Cyprus where Paul made an enemy of an astrologer called Elymas by temporarily blinding him, then north to Galatia. However, Mark left them abruptly at Perga and returned to Jersusalem, perhaps because he was troubled by Paul's plan to preach to the Gentiles.

When Paul was planning his second journey he refused to take Mark with him, taking instead Silas. Paul and Silas travelled to mainland Greece — Phillipi, Thessalonica and Athens — while Barnabas and Mark returned to Cyprus, where Elymas roused the mob and had Barnabas stoned to death. Mark buried the body secretly, putting a copy of St Matthew's Gospel on Barnabas' chest. No one knew where the burial place was until, some four hundred years later, St Barnabas appeared in a dream to the Archibishop of Cyprus telling him where to find the relics, including the Gospel. These were then taken to Constantinople where the Emperor Zeno was so impressed that he conferred three privileges on the Archibishop and his successors — the right to sign their names in red ink, to wear a purple cape adorned with little bells, and to carry a sceptre.

Although St Mark did not appear to have got on well with St Paul, he became a close friend of St Peter. While Peter was busy establishing the Church in Rome, Mark worked as his secretary. Later St Mark is supposed to have settled in Egypt and become the first bishop of Alexandria, one of the most important cities of the Middle East at that time. During Nero's persecution of the Christians, Mark was dragged through the streets, bumping over rough stones, until he died. He was buried in Alexandria, but in 829 some Venetian merchants daringly stole his relics and took them home to Venice. The partly-built church which had been intended as a private chapel for the doges, was turned into a magnificent basilica for the saint's relics.

The Winged Lion of St Mark

St Mark ousted St Theodore (a soldier-saint) as patron saint of Venice. Today, two tall pillars stand in the Piazzetta di San Marco beside the lagoon, one topped by St Theodore and the crocodile which he slew, the other by St Mark's winged lion. This is the only place where they are on equal terms, for everywhere else on the island St Theodore is ignored while the winged lion is inescapable.

Less well known than St Mark's winged lion is the winged ox, symbol of St Luke. The ox is the animal associated with sacrifice and the first incident described in St Luke's Gospel is of the priest, Zacharias, father of John the Baptist, offering his sacrifice at the temple. From his writings Luke appears to have been gentle, sensitive, artistic, and well educated. He is also credited with being an artist and a sculptor; a picture of the Madonna, signed 'Luca' was found in the catacombs and is popularly supposed to be his work. St Luke was the friend, fellow traveller and personal physician of St Paul.

Born at Tarsus of a 'good' Jewish family, Paul (or Saul as he was originally called) could claim to be a Roman citizen. He was trained as a tent-maker but was so interested in theology that he went to Jerusalem to study under the rabbi Galamiel. He became utterly immersed in the Jewish religion and strongly opposed to the Nazarenes, as Christians were called at that time; it was at Antioch some years later that they were first called Christians.

Paul watched Stephen's martyrdom, looking after the garments of the stone-throwing mob. To him it seemed perfectly justified, and there followed such a surge of persecution that Paul (or Saul as he then was) became expert in hunting out the hated Christians. It was while following his anti-Christian pursuits that he was blinded by a great light, and a voice asking 'Saul, Saul, why persecutest thou me?' After three days his sight was restored, and the whole course of his life altered. Paul deserted his former allies and made his way to Jerusalem, anxious to join the other disciples. He became as enthusiastic on the side of the Christians as he had previously been against them. Against tremendous odds he travelled vast distances, over snow-capped mountains, through steaming valleys, across parched desert, on stormy seas, and underwent hair-raising adventures. He was whipped, imprisoned and shipwrecked and under the constant threat of death. He covered almost the whole of modern Greece and Turkey, setting up churches and constantly checking on their progress. His many epistles were intended to keep in contact with those Christian communities which he had established, encouraging them, reproving them, clarifying their problems, or preparing the ground for the journeys he was planning. Paul was not a healthy man, suffering from an incapacitating complaint which caused him agonising pain. He is traditionally described as being short, stout, bandy, bald, beetle-browed and hook-nosed — hardly a handsome character — but he was so eloquent that when he spoke he appeared like an angel.

According to legend St Paul and St Peter were martyred on the same day, the 29th June 67 AD, during Nero's persecution. St Peter was crucified upside down, but St Paul, as a Roman citizen, had his head struck off with a sword. There is a story that the head bounced

St Stephen

three times and at each spot a fountain gushed up. A sword is the symbol of several saints who were martyred in this way, but for St Paul it has a special significance, recognising the way he sheared through all opposition. Undaunted by seemingly insuperable difficulties, he fought to achieve his goal.

Today, when we talk about 'putting away childish things — seeing through a glass darkly — reaping what we sow — heaping coals of fire on someone's head — or being all things to all men' — we are quoting St Paul. When we mention 'a thorn in the flesh — filthy lucre — or the love of money being the root of all evil' — we are also quoting St Paul. He is also quoted in the burial service 'O death where is thy sting?' 'Love suffereth long and is kind' is another quotation frequently used in the marriage service. Finally, another piece of advice often given, 'Let not the sun go down upon your wrath' is worth following today.

There is, however, one quotation which sums up the whole of St Paul's life, and could equally apply to all the other men and women risen to sainthood; 'I have fought a good fight, I have finished my course, I have kept the faith.' What an epitaph!

CHAPTER 3
Early Christian Martyrs

The Romans have the doubtful distinction of being the most outstanding martyr-makers. It is impossible to tell exactly how many Christians they killed; legend nearly always exaggerates and in addition
some chroniclers made genuine mistakes — like taking 'mil', the abbre-
viation for milites (soldiers) to be that for mille (thousands) and so mis-
interpreting the murder of ten soldiers as the slaughter of ten
thousand. Even allowing for this, it is clear that for nearly three hundred years Christians suffered appalling persecution under Roman
rule.

In the early days Christians were hated not only by the Romans but
even more fiercely by the Jews. Miracles worked by the disciples were
ascribed to sorcery, and Paul's determination to include Gentiles in
the Church was the last straw.

The Romans' objections were political rather than religious. With
so many gods of their own, one more was of little importance. They
were not interested in religious quarrels except when they disturbed
the peace. Pontius Pilate was reluctant to crucify Christ, and later St
Paul appeared in front of several Roman governors before the Jews
managed to persuade one to have him executed. Had the Christians
paid lip-service to the Roman gods, acknowledged the divinity of
Caesar and fitted peaceably into society, their strange belief — *'this
mischievous superstition'* as Tacitus called it — might have been
ignored. Their problem was that their religion forebade them to sacrifice to false gods so that, however law-abiding they wished to be, they
kept falling foul of authority.

Until 64 AD Christians were regarded simply as a nuisance. Then, in the year of the great fire of Rome, persecution began in earnest. The wild extravagance of the Emperor Nero had made him intensely unpopular and his callous indifference when Rome was burning, whether or not he actually fiddled at the time, gave rise to the suspicion that he had started the fire himself in order to clear a space for one of his grandiose building projects. He needed a scapegoat and the Christians, misunderstood and disliked as they were, made a convenient one. From this time onwards they were blamed for all sorts of crimes and disasters, even natural catastrophes.

The two best known victims of Nero's persecution were St Peter and St Paul, but many others were thrown to the lions in the arena. This was a recognised form of capital punishment for any serious crime and an economical one as it provided the crowds with entertainment at the same time. Nero added refinements like covering the victims with animal skins and setting packs of wild dogs to pursue them. After suffering unimaginable tortures, the surviving Christians were burnt to death. Tacitus said that the flames of their martyrdom provided *'nightly illuminations.'*

Under Vespasian (69-79AD) there was no deliberate policy of persecution. Compared with Nero he was wise, just and humane, and yet he accepted as a matter of course that criminals, including Christians, should be thrown to the animals in the arena. He was followed by his two sons, first Titus, who in 70 AD had destroyed the Temple of Jerusalem after the Jewish rising, and then Domitian who for greed and cruelty rivalled Nero. The only subjects who approved of him were his soldiers to whom he promised excessive pay increases! These, and his lavish entertainments and expensive building projects, had to be financed somehow, and once again the Christians provided an easy target. Domitian accused them of evading the temple tax which had to be paid by all Jews, even though there was no longer a temple. St John the Evangelist, although very old, was still alive in Domitian's time. It is said that after trying unsuccessfully to dispose of John by having him boiled in oil, the emperor exiled him to Patmos.

As Gibbon points out in his 'Decline and Fall of the Roman Empire', Christians generally fared better under the dissolute emper-

St Christopher carrying the Christ-child

ors like Commodus (180-193) who had no time to spare for religion, than under the good ones like Trajan (98-177) who, in their determination to maintain law and order, insisted on conformity. Christians stubbornly chose torture and death rather than being forced to fulfil seemingly simple requirements. They would not deny their faith, no matter what the cost.

St Clement, St Eustace and St Ignatius were all martyred during Trajan's persecution. St Clement, fourth bishop of Rome, had narrowly escaped martyrdom under Domitian. Under Trajan he was sentenced to hard labour in the marble quarries of the Crimea and was eventually put to death by being tied to an anchor and thrown into the sea. His symbol is an anchor, sometimes with fishes for good measure, and he is the patron saint of many places having a maritime connection. Trinity House was originally called the Guild of the Holy Trinity and St Clement.

St Eustace was an army officer who, like St Hubert some six hundred years later, was converted while out hunting by seeing a stag with a crucifix between its horns. A voice warned him that if he followed Christ he would suffer great tribulation. He accepted this and the prophecy came true; he and his family lost all their possessions and were carried off by pirates. Eventually he was reinstated in Trajan's army and played a conspicuous part in a successful campaign but he refused to join in the victory celebrations giving thanks to the heathen gods. He and his wife and two sons were shut up in a huge brazen effigy of a bull and roasted to death.

The third victim, St Ignatius, is generally supposed to have been the child whom Jesus set in the midst of his disciples saying, '*of such is the Kingdom of Heaven.*' By Trajan's time he was bishop of Antioch and an old man. He was arrested at Antioch and taken to Rome where he was eventually devoured by wild animals in the Colosseum. On the long journey to Rome his captors allowed him to write a number of letters, seven of which have been preserved. Most were to other Christian communities, but one was to Polycarp, the young bishop of Smyrna whom he had just met. Many years later, in the time of Antoninus Pius, St Polycarp too was martyred, burnt to death for refusing to blaspheme against Jesus who, he said, had cared for him for eighty-six years. St Polycarp's tomb was the first at which a service of celebration was held annually on his feast day.

The Antonines, Antoninus Pius (138-161) and his nephew-by-marriage Marcus Aurelius (161-180) were arguably the best of the Roman Emperors, but not from the Christian point of view. Instead of the usual embroidered legend there is an authentic account of some terrible events which took place in 177 AD — a letter sent by eye-witnesses to the churches of Asia and recorded by the 4th-century ecclesiastical historian Eusebius. Because of a misunderstanding of their beliefs the Christians were accused of incest and cannibalism, but a young slave-girl called Blandina, kept repeating courageously, '*I am a Christian and we do nothing vile.*' As well as Blandina, forty-seven other victims are named, including a 15 year old boy called Pontius and the 90 year old bishop Pothinus. After being tortured they were sent to the arena where they were attacked by starving lions, leopards and bears. Encouraged by Blandina they steadfastly refused to renounce their faith, glorying in their suffering which would assure them of eternal life. The atrocities lasted for a week. Blandina was kept until last and then, entangled in a net, was thrown to a bull and gored to death.

The two-year reign of Decius, who was killed in battle in 251, was disastrous for Christians. Determined to restore Rome's 'public virtue' he issued an edict compelling every citizen to offer a sacrifice to the state gods before official witnesses, who would then issue a certificate. The punishment for nonconformity was death. Some Christians gave in and made the required sacrifice, others bribed the commissioners to issue a certificate, but many more suffered torture and martyrdom rather than comply.

Among probable victims of the Decian persecutian were St Denis, patron saint of France, Valentine who is commemorated by St Valentine's Day, and Christopher, patron saint of travellers. The figure of a man carrying a child on his shoulders is the most widely recognised of saintly images, and he must be very hard-worked if he keeps an eye on all those who hopefully carry St Christopher medallions! Sadly, both he and Valentine are now omitted from the Church calendar because of doubt about their authenticity. Legend has it that Christopher was a giant whose greatest desire was to serve the most powerful master in the world. He had considerable trouble deciding who this could be for everyone he tried conceded that someone else was more powerful. A great king admitted that he feared the devil, and after a spell of serving Satan, Christopher found that even he trembled at the name of Jesus.

While continuing his search, he went to live on the bank of a broad river and a hermit suggested that he might put his great strength to good use by carrying people across it. One night he was awakened by a boy asking for this service. Christopher hoisted him on to his shoulders and waded out into the water, but somehow the crossing was harder than usual. The child seemed so heavy that Christopher, struggling, said he felt as if he were carrying the whole world on his shoulders. 'You are,' said the boy. 'And He who made it.' Only then did Christopher realise that he was carrying the Christchild and that his search was at an end.

Another very popular but more authentic saint is St Lawrence of Rome. Both he and the pope whom he served were martyred during the reign of Valerian (253-260). Born in Aragon of a noble Spanish family, as a very young man St Lawrence went to Rome to study. He was greatly loved for his humility and genuine care for the poor. Pope Sixtus I made him archdeacon and entrusted him with the church treasure. When the prefect of the city ordered him to hand it over, St Lawrence called together all the poor and sick and presented them to the prefect saying, '*Behold the church's treasure.*' Both pope and archdeacon were arrested. While in prison St Lawrence converted his gaoler, Hippolytus, who was also martyred. St Sixtus was beheaded and three days afterwards St Lawrence was roasted on a gridiron. Legend claims that he faced this horrible death so calmly that he was able to say to his torturers, "Turn me over; I'm cooked on that side." He is today the patron saint of rotisseurs.

The second half of the third century was a fairly peaceful one for Christians. The last systematic persecution was carried out in the final years of the reign of Diocletian (284-306). An extremely able ruler, he was also, until a few years before his abdication, a tolerant one. Then, partly under the influence of his associates Galerius and Maximian, and partly because of his own convictions, he turned against the Christians. On the festival of the god Terminus, he issued an edict compell-

St Vincent — Lisbon Coat of Arms

ing everyone to sacrifice to the state gods, on pain of torture and death. Churches were to be destroyed and all Christian writing burned.

Sebastian, a soldier in the imperial guard, suffered under this edict. He had been a friend of Diocletian before the latter's change of heart, but for refusing to make the ritual sacrifice, he was tied naked to a tree and shot at by archers who left him for dead. There was still a spark of life in him, however, and a widow called Irene revived him and nursed him back to health. Instead of remaining safely in hiding he insisted on returning to the palace to confront Diocletian. Bitter words were exchanged and the emperor, furious at Sebastian's accusations, had him beaten to death with clubs. It is the shooting episode which has appealed to artists and also made Sebastian the Patron saint of archers, arrowsmiths and pinmakers. He was much invoked in the Middle Ages against the plague and other diseases which struck suddenly and inexplicably, like arrows shot by an unseen hand.

St Vincent, a saint much honoured in Spain and Portugal, was a deacon of Saragossa, who unflinchingly endured torture and death during Diocletian's persecution. His body was tied to a millstone and flung into the sea, but the tide carried it ashore and buried it in a shallow grave. Many years later its hiding place was revealed to Christians who took it first to Valencia, then, when they were driven out by Saracens, to the promontory afterwards called Cape St Vincent. Ravens who had followed the relics on their sea journey, remained with them at the Cape, and again followed them on their subsequent removal to Lisbon. St Vincent is the patron saint of Lisbon and his ravens appear in the city's coat-of-arms.

St Nicholas and St George, both dealt with more fully in a later chapter, also lived in the time of Diocletian. St George was a Roman soldier martyred at Lydda for defying the emperor's edict. Very little is known about him, but he may have been the man who contemptuously tore down the edict as soon as it was nailed up, and trampled it underfoot, — a daring act of defiance. The martyr's cult was brought back to England by crusaders whom he is said to have helped, and he became the patron saint of English soldiers and his name became their battle cry. He was extremely popular in the Middle Ages, the patron saint of many guilds, and the hero of mumming plays. Edward III made him official patron saint of England, and instituted in his honour the Order of the Garter, whose members still walk in solemn procession to St George's chapel in Windsor on 23rd April, the Saint's feast day.

It is difficult to extract the few grains of fact from the mass of legend that surrounds St George. The same could be said of his contemporary, St Nicholas. He was, almost certainly, a bishop of Myra in Asia Minor. He may have been tortured under Diocletian but he died a natural death and was buried in his own cathedral. Later his relics were stolen by Italian merchants and taken to Bari in south-east Italy.

During the 3rd and early 4th centuries there lived a number of remarkable girl saints who all had one thing in common — their determination to remain virgins and to dedicate themselves entirely to Christ. One of these, St Agatha, lived in Catania in Sicily in about 250 AD. The prefect Quintianus fell in love with her and was so dismayed when she rejected his advances that he denounced her as a Christian. One of the frightful tortures she endured was having her breasts cut off. In early illustrations she was sometimes shown carrying them on a dish. They were later mistaken by some for bells, making her the patron saint of bell-founders and by others for bread rolls, from which grew the custom of blessing bread on a dish on her feast day, the 5th February. On this day her silver sarcophagus is carried in procession through the streets of Catania, commemorating the occasion when she saved the town from destruction. About a year after her death Mount Etna erupted, and a tide of molten lava threatened to engulf the town. Carrying her veil, and praying for her aid, a group of inhabitants stood in the path of the lava stream. It turned aside and Catania was saved.

About fifty years later another Sicilian girl, Lucy of Syracuse, also rejected a wealthy suitor because she had made a vow of chastity. Soon afterwards she took her mother, who was seriously ill, on a pilgrimage to St Agatha's tomb at Catania. The saint appeared, healed the sick woman, and encouraged Lucy to keep her vow. As in Agatha's case the rejected suitor denounced Lucy as a Christian. She endured many tortures without weakening. Her eyes were put out, but miraculously restored, more beautiful than ever. Because of this she is often portrayed holding her eyes on a dish and is invoked by people suffering from eye-trouble. Perhaps because of the resemblance of her name to the Latin word for light, *lux*, she is associated with festivals of light, particularly in Sweden where her feast day, the 13th December, is a time of special celebration.

St Agnes of Rome was a contemporary of St Lucy. She was only thirteen years old when a young officer, son of a Roman prefect, asked to marry her. She refused on the grounds that she had already promised herself to Christ. Because of her open avowal of Christianity she was condemned to be publicly burnt to death, but the fire went out and could not be rekindled so she was stabbed in the throat. Subsequently she appeared to her parents holding a white lamb and this is how she is usually portrayed. On her feast day, the 21st January, two white lambs are blessed in her church in Rome and from their wool is woven the pallia worn by archbishops. Some of the details of her story are probably imaginary but she undoubtedly existed and was martyred at about the age of thirteen.

Around the same time, a beautiful young girl called Dorothy, who lived at Caesarea in Cappadocia, was also in danger of her life for refusing to sacrifice to heathen gods. Theophilus, a young lawyer, tried to save her by proposing marriage but she declined his help, saying that she would gladly endure any suffering that would bring her to Christ. Hurt by her rejection, he mockingly asked her to send him fruit and flowers when she reached the heavenly gardens. After her execution, a child appeared before Theophilus and offered him a basket of apples and roses. Following this proof he too became a Christian and was martyred in his turn.

*   *   *

On the whole things were not too bad for Christians in Britain, especially under the governor Constantius, who was a wise and tolerant man. His son Constantine was proclaimed co-emperor in York in 306 while on duty there with the army. He fell out with his co-emperor Maxentius and there was a fierce batter between them at Milvian Bridge in 312. Constantine later told the historian Eusebius that on the

St Lucy with her eyes on a dish

The Banner of St Vincent

afternoon before the battle he saw a great cross in the sky and the words *'in hoc vinces'* — 'In this you will conquer.' That night in a dream he was told to adopt the *'Chi-Ro'* symbol as his standard. He obeyed, won a decisive victory and was converted.

Both Constantine and his mother, St Helena, whom he made Empress, openly embraced the Christian religion. They built many churches and made Jerusalem a place of pilgrimage. St Helena is best remembered for her dream in which she was told where to find the Cross on which Christ was crucified.

The Edict of Milan issued by Constantine and his co-emperor Licinius granted religious toleration and brought to an end the long Roman persecution.

We have to return to Rome for St Cecilia. On her wedding day she told her bridegroom, Valerian, that she had made a vow of chastity! Her arguments were so convincing that she converted not only Valerian but also his brother Tibertius. All three were martyred about the same time, Cecilia by suffocation. Legend says that she was a talented musician, so she became the patron saint of musicians, and her symbol is a portable organ.

St Catherine of Alexandria provides a slight variation on the same theme. In her case it was not a rejected suitor who caused her death but a provoked emperor. She seemed to have everything, wealth, position, beauty and brains, but above all a steadfast faith. She had not been brought up as a Christian, but became one as a result of her studies. She openly criticised the Emperor Maxentius for enforcing the worship of false gods. Struck by her courage and beauty, he tried to reason with her himself, but she made nonsense of all his arguments. He sent for his fifty most learned counsellors and Catherine defeated them with equal ease. Understandably furious, the emperor had them all executed as a useless lot, and Catherine was to be put to death in the most painful way possible, by being torn to pieces on a wheel whose two halves revolved in opposite directions. At the crucial moment an angel appeared and broke the wheel and Catherine met a speedier death by having her head struck off with a sword. More angels appeared and carried her body to the top of Mount Sinai, where a great monastery was later built and where her relics are still preserved.

Many churches were dedicated to her, especially in the hills and high places, but in spite of her popularity she was recently removed from the official Calendar of Saints for lack of authenticity. She appears in a great many stained glass windows, usually with the wheel of her torture and sometimes with the sword of her execution as well. A round or rose window is cometimes called a Catherine window, and of course she also has a firework named after her, the 'Catherine Wheel.'

There are many other virgin saints, including St Faith (St Foy) who lived at Agen in France and whose dedications in Britain include a chapel in the crypt of St Paul's cathedral, and St Ursula, martyred with eleven other virgins, a number somehow misinterpreted and popularly accepted as eleven thousand.

St Ursula and her maidens, although particularly venerated in Cologne where they are said to have been martyred, are thought to have come originally from Britain. The first Christain martyred on British soil was St Alban. Dates quoted for his execution vary from 209 to 303 AD, but is seems likely that it took place during Diocletian's persecution near the latter date. He was born at Verulamium (now St Albans) of Roman parents and sent to Rome to study. After a spell in the army he returned to his home town. One day he gave shelter to a fugitive priest and was so impressed by him that he took the priest's place when the soldiers arrived to arrest him. The historian Bede describes how he was executed on Holmhurst Hill where the great abbey was later built.

Reliquary of St Faith (St Foy)

CHAPTER 4

Doctors of the Church

Constantine the Great made Christianity respectable by embracing it himself; Theodosius the Great made Christianity compulsory.

Theodosius (347-395) was the last ruler of an undivided Roman Empire. After his day, East and West began to go their separate ways in both politics and religion. Although Rome in the west and Constantinople, Constantine's New Rome, in the East, maintained contact for another four hundred years, the Greek-speaking Byzantine church and the Latin-speaking Roman one were developing along different lines.

In the West the Bishop of Rome, 'papa', the pope, was the undisputed head of the Church. With the danger of persecution removed and Christianity recognised as the official religion, it seemed that everything would now run smoothly.

What happened, in fact, was just the opposite. The glorious unquestioning faith of the martyrs gave way to theological arguments. Arianism. Nestorianism, Donatism, Pelagianism and a plethora of other '-isms' questioned the true nature of God, the Trinity and the divinity of Christ. They were all condemned by the Church as heretical. It was no longer enough to be simply a Christain; it seemed almost worse to be a heretic who presumably had the wrong views about Christian doctrine than a pagan who had none at all. It was a time of bitter dissension within the Church and, to make matters worse, with the crumbling of the Roman Empire, hordes of pagan tribes were sweeping down from the North, trampling over Europe and into North Africa.

St Jerome

In this age of heresies the four saints who sorted out the tangle and who later became known as the Four Doctors of the western church were Ambrose, Augustine of Hippo, Jerome and Gregory the Great. They often appear together in wood carvings and stained glass windows, St Ambrose carrying a beehive, St Augustine holding a heart pierced with an arrow, and St Gregory, the only pope among them, wearing his papal tiara. When he appears with his three companions, St Jerome usually wears his cardinal's round flat hat, but artists enjoyed painting him in his more dramatic role as a desert hermit clad only in rags, in a wild desolate setting with his lion lurking nearby.

St Jerome was undoubtedly one of the greatest scholars among the saints, but also one of the least likeable. He was, to put it bluntly, often rude and bad-tempered, but he had the virtue of getting cross with himself as well as with everyone else. He must have had some magnetic quality because he inspired great devotion among his friends and followers, especially among the ladies of whom there was an embarrassing number.

His real name was Eusebius Hieronymous and he was born in Dalmatia in about 342. He first studied law in Rome, but after being baptised at the age of twenty, devoted himself to theology. He went off to the Syrian desert, where for many years he lived a life of prayer and fasting among the desert fathers. 'My hideous emaciated limbs were covered with sackcloth, my skin was dry and black and my flesh was almost wasted away,' he says.

In spite of his self-mortification, or perhaps in further pursuit of it, he set about learning Hebrew and, with his fine brain and intense determination, soon mastered it. In 382 he went to Rome to become secretary to the pope, St Damasus, who ordered him to translate the Bible into Latin. He translated the Old Testament from Hebrew, and for the New Testament compared and revised existing Latin and Greek texts. His 'Vulgate' as it was later called, became the standard Bible of the Roman Catholic church.

It was a mammoth task and only partially completed when the pope died. Jerome returned to the East, followed by some of the women who had studied with him in Rome. One of them, St Paula, was very wealthy, and together they founded a monastery, a convent and a school in Bethlehem. The translation was completed in 404, but Jerome was still involved in writing religious works and in making scathing attacks on the heresy of Pelagianism. Constantly in the background was a fear of invasion, and in 410 when Alaric and his Visigoths sacked Rome, the peace of Jerome's monastery was disturbed by refugees seeking shelter.

Pope Sixtus V is supposed to have remarked to St Jerome, on seeing a picture of him beating his breast with a stone, that without such self-mortification he would never have been considered a saint. Legend attributes a gentler side to his character in the story of the lion which limped up to him with a thorn in its paw and, when he removed it, remained with him as his devoted bodyguard.

The Beehive of St Ambrose

St Ambrose was as gentle and persuasive as St Jerome was brusque and vituperative. There is a story that when he was a very small boy, Ambrose fell asleep while playing in the garden. His mother was shocked at finding him with a bee (some say a whole swarm!) crawling in and out of his mouth. It flew away without stinging him and was taken as a sign that his words would always be as sweet as honey.

Ambrose was born in about 340 AD at Trèves in West Germany (his father was a prefect of Gaul) and like so many other wealthy young men he went to Rome to study law. He proved an able and popular administrator, and when the bishop of Milan died he was called upon to preside over the stormy election of a successor. Somewhat to his surprise he found himself elected to the position. As bishop he needed all his tact and honey-sweet eloquence, not only for converting the pagans but for combating the Arian heretics. Theirs was the first and most widespread of the heresies. In 325 AD when Constantine held the first-ever council of Christian churches at Nicaea, the two opposing factions were led by Arius and Athanasius, both from Alexandria. The main contention was about the relationship of Jesus and God; were they 'of one substance', in which case they would be equal, or 'of like substance'? Arius argued that the son could not possibly be equal to his father, St Athanasius asserted that he was. St Athanasius won the day and the followers of Arius were declared heretics, but there were a great many of them including, in Ambrose's day, the empress-regent Justina.

The saint soon proved that his mellifluous tongue could be razor-sharp when necessary. He not only defied Justina's order to hand over a church to the Arians for their Easter celebrations, but dared to excommunicate the emperor Theodore — for having allowed the massacre of some rioters. Theodore may have felt that the killing was justified because the rioters had murdered their governor, but after eight months he gave in and made public penance at Milan cathedral.

Ambrose's legal training stood him in good stead and churches far afield appealed to him to settle their disputes. He was, naturally, an eloquent orator and introduced the use of hymns, several of which he wrote himself. He had a great influence on all whom he met, and his most important convert was undoubtedly St Augustine of Hippo.

While St Ambrose began life with all the advantages of a happy childhood, the circumstances of St Augustine's upbringing were certainly not conducive to sainthood. He had a disagreeable pagan father, whom he hated, and a domineering Christian mother, St Monica, whom he adored. He seems when young to have been as 'crazy and mixed-up' as any modern youth. His mother was ambitious for him and tried too hard to force her religious convictions on him. She was greatly distressed by his loose living and strongly disapproved of his mistress, by whom he had a son, Adeodatus.

They lived at Thagaste in Algeria, and Augustine, who turned out to be a brilliant teacher, set up schools there and later at Carthage. He was invited to teach in Rome and then took up a government post in

The Wheel of St Catherine of Alexandria

Milan where he came under the influence of St Ambrose, by whom both he and his son were later baptised, much to the delight of St Monica who had followed him to Italy.

Augustine admitted that at first he had listened with pleasure to St Ambrose's eloquent sermons without paying much attention to the subject matter. Then, so it is said, one day while he was sitting in his garden, a voice bade him take up his Bible and read — *'Iolle, lege!'* — and his subsequent study of the Scriptures brought conviction. On his return to North Africa he was made bishop of Hippo (now Bone) where he remained for 35 years until his death in 430 AD. He spent his time battling against persistent heresies and under the constant threat of pagan invasion — at the time of his death the Visigoths were at the very gates of Hippo — and yet he retained his unwavering faith.

The agony of indecision Augustine went through while searching for the truth (symbolised by his attribute, a pierced heart) helped him to set out his ideas clearly once he had made up his mind. He was a brilliant and prolific writer — two of his books, *Confessions* and *The City of God*, are still regarded as classics — and is considered to be one of the greatest theologians of all time.

Even Augustine thought that his *City of God*, which took thirteen years to write, was a bit long — twenty-two books of profound theological argument! *Confessions* is also a philosophical work but is interesting for his views on the development of personality. He describes how a baby first notices objects and gets frustrated when it wants to play with sunbeams or the fire's dancing flames and is fobbed off with a toy. From his own memory he tells how he learnt the names of objects and how to put sentences together by the language which teachers today would call the 'direct method.' Being rather spoilt at home by his devoted mother, he had a tough time when he went to school, and was in constant trouble over his idleness. "I loved not study and hated to be forced to it," he says. "Yet I was forced and this was well done towards me, for unless forced I had not learnt" — an unpopular theory these days but it certainly paid off in Augustine's case.

He left school at fifteen and, having nothing to do, got into bad company and spent his time drinking, gambling, womanising, watching chariot races and going to the theatre. He admits to being lazy, greedy and dishonest. Like many modern shoplifters he and his companions stole for excitement rather than from need. One night they stripped a pear tree and then threw all the fruit to the pigs. However, once he had seen the error of his ways he tried to analyse his motives and this led to a study of right and wrong. Altogether he wrote 117 books, an extraordinary output, and had a more profound influence on Church doctrine than anyone except St Paul.

The last of the Big Four, Gregory the Great, lived about two centuries after the others. The first and most famous of sixteen popes of the same name, he was the first pope to call himself 'the servant of the servants of God,' a title that has been used ever since.

At a most difficult time, with Lombards rampaging all over Italy and the emperor's authority waning, he was the right man for the job. Born in Rome of a wealthy patrician family, with a pope for one of his great-grandfathers, he started with plenty of advantages. He was well educated, clever, deeply pious, a good organiser and a skilled diplo-

St Martin dividing his cloak

mat, but managed to retain a sense of humility in his relationships with others which made him well liked.

While a senior magistrate in Rome, Gregory founded the Benedictine abbey of St Andrews and, drawn to the monastic life, later entered it as a simple monk. He would have liked to have been a missionary, especially after seeing the fair-haired, blue-eyed boys for sale in the market place when he is supposed to have said, 'Not Angles but angels,' but his importance as adviser to the pope precluded this. When he himself reluctantly became pope, in 590, he was determined that one of his tasks would be to convert the fellow-countrymen of the slave-boys. He sent forty monks from the abbey of St Andrews under the leadership of St Augustine (not the saint of Hippo) to re-establish Christianity in England. In his fourteen years of office he restored a measure of peace to troubled Italy by his shrewd negotiations with the Lombards, and made the Church strong and respected. When he died in 604 he was canonised by popular acclaim.

In addition, to the Big Four, a few other saints have been declared 'doctors of the church'; Bernard of Clairvaux, for instance, the 'honey-sweet doctor', sometimes confused with St Ambrose as he too has a beehive as his symbol. St Bernard preached the second Crusade and established the Cistercian Order.

St Hilary of Poitiers, who died in 368, was given his official title of doctor in 1851, although St Augustine had already called him 'the illustrious doctor'. The Hilary Term of law courts and universities is so called because it begins on or near his feast day, the 14th January. He is best known for his fight against Arianism. After being made bishop of his home town, Poitiers, he was exiled by the Arian emperor Constantius II. During his four years of exile he travelled as far as Constantinople, and on his return to Poitiers, was given a great welcome. He had a profound influence on all with whom he came into contact.

Perhaps better known than St Hilary is his friend and disciple, Martin of Tours. St Martin's-in-the-Fields is one of the many churches dedicated to him. St Martin was born in Pannonia, now Southern

Horseshoe-studded door of St Martin's Church, Chablis

Hungary, where his soldier father was serving. Soon afterwards the family was transferred to Pavia, Northern Italy. At the age of ten Martin became a catechumen, against his parents' wishes, and at fifteen he joined the army as a cavalry officer. He lived frugally so that he could afford to give alms to the poor, and one day when he had no money to give to a shivering beggar, he cut his cloak in half and gave this to him. That night he had a vision of Christ wearing the garment he had given away — a popular subject for pictures. Why he didn't give the beggar the complete cloak is not explained!

He asked to be relieved of his army service because of his conscientious objection to killing, and joined St Hilary at Poitiers. He too was hounded by the Arians, but after much travelling and a spell as a hermit in Milan he became bishop of Tours where he remained for fifty successful years. Instead of living in the town, he settled at Marmoutier, a quiet spot nearby where he founded a monastery. He travelled all over his diocese, on foot, on horseback (often on donkeyback) or by boat, and was greatly loved by the people of Gaul. St Martin is the patron saint of knights and horsemen. Horseshoes were sometimes nailed to the doors of churches dedicated to him as a votive offering indicating the completion of a vow.

Leo the Great, proclaimed a Doctor of the Church by Pope Benedict XIV in 1754, was not only a good theologian but also a man of great personal courage. He was pope from 440 to 461 when Rome was under constant threat from barbarian tribes. While the Huns, fearsome horsemen from the steppes, were advancing on the city, Leo went to meet their leader, Attila, and persuaded him to turn back. Legend adds that he was helped by a vision of St Peter and St Paul which appeared in the sky, a scene later painted by Raphael.

In 455, only three years after being spared by the Huns, Rome was threatened by Vandals. Once again Leo went out to meet the leader, this time at the gates of the city. Gaiseric would not be turned away as Attila had been, but he restrained his troops and Rome suffered only a fortnight's looting instead of the expected massacre.

St Thomas Aquinas with his Star

The eastern Church also had its Four Doctors — St Athanasius, St Basil, another St Gregory, and St John Chrysostom.

St Athanasius, a deacon of Alexandria, made a name for himself at the Council of Nicaea in 325. He had gone there simply as chaplain to this bishop, but spoke out so strongly against Arianism that the heresy was officially condemned. Three years later he became bishop of Alexandria, and remained so for forty-six years, although he spent a total of sixteen years in exile. He was physically small, but very courageous and mentally brilliant. His writings were regarded as so important that several centuries later a monk advised his fellows if they ever found a book of his and had nothing to copy it on, to "Write it on your shirts!"

Basil the Great was born into a saintly family — grandmother, father, mother, one sister and two brothers were all saints. As a young man he visited monasteries all over the East and joined one himself for five years; he had as profound an influence on monastic life in the East as St Benedict did in the West. As bishop of Caesarea he was in constant conflict with the Arian emperor Valens, but refused to be browbeaten. It is for his writings that he has since become famous, but at the time he was most appreciated for his practical help to the poor and sick. He built at Caesarea what was virtually a new town with houses, a hospital, a hospice for travellers and a church. He died in 378, three years after St Athanasius, at the age of fifty.

St Gregory Nazianzus was a friend of St Basil's. In spite of being very shy and retiring, he was so eloquent a preacher and knowledgeable a writer that he was known as 'the Theologian.'

Last of the four eastern doctors was St John Chrysostom. The nickname, not given to him until after his death, means 'golden-mouthed,' and because of his wonderful sermons he is the patron saint of preachers.

He was born in Antioch in Syria in 347, the only son of a high-ranking army officer. His father died when he was a baby and his mother, only twenty when she was widowed, brought him up as a Christian. He was baptised at the age of eighteen and wanted to become a hermit, but his mother persuaded him to wait until after her death. Then he went up into the mountains and spent six solitary years in prayer and study. On his return to Antioch he quickly acquired a reputation as an outstanding preacher and crowds flocked to hear him, but his out-spokenness made him many enemies, especially among those whom he accused of misusing their wealth and power. Soon after being made archbishop of Constantinople, he was exiled by the emperor. After three difficult years he was ordered to move even further away, to a remote spot on the Black Sea, but he died of exhaustion on the way. His last words were, "Glory be to God for everything. Amen."

He was, we are told, a rather spidery little man, small, pale, and bald, but he made a tremendous impact on the Church, with East and West. His main concern was to explain the Bible so that everyone could understand it and relate it to everday life. In this he was so successful that today, nearly sixteen centuries later, his sermons are still relevant.

The oustanding medieval theologian, St Thomas Aquinas, who lived some 800 years after the early Doctors of the Church, is often called the 'Angelic Doctor'. He was born at Roccasecca in Italy in 1225 and in his late teens joined the Dominican Order in Naples. The idea of his becoming a mendicant friar so shocked his aristocratic family that they kidnapped him and kept him at home for a year. Further studies at Cologne and Paris earned him the degree of Master of Theology and a reputation for remarkable scholarship but did nothing to alter his humility. A clear thinker and prolific writer, he produced weighty treatises which enlightened a confused church. His symbol is, appropriately, a star shedding rays of light.

CHAPTER 5

The Voyagers

While the great Doctors of the Church were writing learned treatises and hammering out official doctrines, Christianity in Britain was in danger of disappearing, swamped by invading pagan tribes — Saxons from the lowlands of the Elbe region, Picts from Scotland, and Scots from Ireland — Christians were also being misled by the plausible heresy of a man called Pelagius.

Pelagius was born somewhere in Britain — there is one theory that he was a Welsh monk called Morgan — but we know nothing definite about him until his arrival in Rome to study. He remained there for about twenty years, producing a number of important theological works, but left in 410 when the city was threatened by Alaric and his Visigoths. In the course of his travels he went to North Africa where he met St Augustine of Hippo, and to Jerusalem where he came into conflict with St Jerome. St Augustine, with his balanced outlook, was able to admire the integrity and scholarship of Pelagius, although he disagreed most strongly with his beliefs, but St Jerome had no such constraint. This fiery-tempered saint was then living in his monastery in Bethlehem and if they came face to face, as they probably did, there must have been some stormy scenes.

Pelagius did not, of course, consider himself a heretic. He sincerely believed he was a true Christian, and in his writings bitterly attacked the Arian heresy. What he could not accept in the Church's teaching was the doctrine of original sin and the need for divine grace; he believed man could become good by his own efforts. He had a tremen-

66   *An Apostle — Church of St. Sernin, Toulouse*

dous number of followers — the Pope himself at one time supported him — and although he was eventually excommunicated, his influence was widespread and long-lasting. Pelagianism took a firm hold in Britain and by 429 conventional Christianity had reached a low ebb. Pope Celestine I decided that something must be done and sent two bishops, St Germanus of Auxerre and Lupus of Troyes, to stamp out the heresy.

St Germanus, born of wealthy Gallo-Roman parents in Gaul about 378, followed the usual pattern of going to Rome to study law. There he married and practised as a barrister, becoming so well known that the emperor appointed him as governor of Armorica and Nervica, based at his home town of Auxerre, a post which he held with great success. The bishop, Amator, was so convinced that Germanus was the right man to succeed him that he tricked him into promising to do so; when Germanus followed a crowd into church, Amator seized him, cut his hair short and put the bishop's robe on him. After Amator's death in 418, Germanus reluctantly fulfilled his promise, but carried out the office with his usual dedication and competence.

He had been bishop for eleven years when he was sent to Britain. On the way he passed through Nanterre and spotted among the crowds waiting for his blessing the little girl called Geneviève who was later to become the patron saint of Paris. There is a story that as he blessed her he noticed a small coin with a cross on it lying in the dust at her feet. He picked it up and gave it to her, telling her to keep it to remind her of that day. Long afterwards it became the custom to distribute bread rolls marked with a cross on her feast day.

As soon as Germanus and Lupus arrived in Britain, they began preaching against the Pelagian heresy. Eventually they had a public confrontation with the heretic leaders and defeated them in argument so convincingly that they were acclaimed by the crowd and word spread that the Pelagians were wrong.

Germanus not only won a moral victory over the heretics but helped the Britons to win a literal one over the pagan invaders. On the eve of Easter, 430, while Germanus and Lupus were holding a service of baptism in Cheshire, they received an urgent appeal for help. Saxons and Picts had joined forces, sailing up the River Dee and devastating the surrounding land. Germanus took command, leading the troops up into the hills and making them hide above a narrow valley through which the pirates would pass. As they entered the defile, the Britons rushed down on them, yelling "Alleluia!" at the top of their voices. The sudden unexpected attack and the cries, echoing and re-echoing round the hills, so unnerved the invaders that they fled. This bloodless victory, the 'Alleluia Victory' as it was called, made Germanus even more famous. Before returning to Gaul he gave thanks at the tomb of St Alban, the first British martyr.

Then followed fourteen years of comparative peace but very hard work in his see of Auxerre. In 444 he received another summons to Britain to quell a brief outbreak of Pelagianism. Four years later, although old and tired, he travelled to Ravenna to plead with the emperor on behalf of the people of Armorica. While there, he fell ill, and knowing that he would soon die, begged the emperor's mother, Placidia, to send his body home. He died on 31st July 448 and Placidia had his remains sent to Auxerre where they were buried with great public mourning.

While he was bishop, St Germanus trained many young priests, one of whom went on to become the famous missionary to Ireland, St Patrick. In his turn St Patrick inspired other missionary saints who rekindled the flame of Christianity in the north of England and kept it alive in the Celtic west — in Wales, Cornwall and Brittany — when most of Britain, after 400 years of Roman rule, had again slipped into the hands of pagan tribes.

Of all the missionary monks the one who is supposed to have travelled furthest (without apparently achieving very much) is Brendan the Voyager. Born in Kerry about 486, he was brought up by St Ita, an abbess who ran a boys' school. When he grew up he became a monk and founded an abbey, but he is best known for the tales of his adventurous voyages.

The first lasted seven years, and he and his companions had many extraordinary adventures, including the celebration of Easter communion on a whale's back, and a meeting with Judas Iscariot who was having his weekly breather from Hell! Apparently, Judas was allowed to spend one day in seven sitting on a rock washed by ice-cold waves.

The travellers encountered monsters and whirlpools and impenetrable fogs, and when at last they reached a beautiful flower-strewn island they received a divine command not to land but to turn round and sail home again! St Brendan obeyed, only to be ordered by St Ita to build a bigger and better boat capable of carrying him to the Land of Promise.

When it was ready they set sail again, first north, then west, and after another seven-year voyage, during which they saw icebergs and an island covered with white birds, they finally reached their goal. After spending some time in the Land of Promise, they returned home bringing seeds and precious stones to prove that they had been there.

Discounting its fantastic aspects, there is a strong theory that the story could be basically true and that St Brendan crossed the Atlantic. In May, 1976, an enthusiastic crew of four, (two English, one Irish, one Danish) set out to see if it could have been done. They sailed from Co. Kerry in a 32-foot leather boat similar to St Brendan's except for its modern navigational aids. The leather was kept waterproof by being greased with tallow and cod oil, and the boat stood up to the journey remarkably well. It reached Iceland safely and, after wintering there, sailed again in May and arrived off Newfoundland in late June 1977. So perhaps St Brendan really did discover the New World 900 years before Columbus!

St Ninian was probably a contemporary of St Germanus, but we know little about him except that he was a British monk trained in Rome, and that on his way back to Britain he spent some time with St Martin at Tours. He settled in Galloway in southern Scotland, converted the local Picts (including their ruler) and established a Christian settlement at Whithorn, retiring to a nearby cave whenever he needed to meditate.

St Columba, born in Donegal about 521, also worked among the Picts. He was, we are told, tall, strong, handsome (with fair skin, dark hair and grey eyes), wise, kind and cheerful, with a powerful and melodious voice. He was of royal blood and well-educated, mainly by the aged bishop, St Finnian. It is possible that he had always intended being a priest, but legend invents an explanation of his action. On a visit to his old tutor, he was so impressed by a beautiful Psalter that he asked permission to copy it. Finnian refused, but Columba could not resist the temptation to borrow it and copy it secretly. He was delighted with his work until Finnian found out and claimed the copy too. After much argument they appealed to the king who gave judgement in Finnian's favour saying, 'To every cow her calf, to every book its copy.' Columba, extremely angry, stirred up his clan, the O'Neills, and in the ensuing battle 3,000 men were slain.

Columba was shattered with remorse and vowed that he would spend the rest of his life praying for forgiveness and would leave the country he had wronged and never see it again. It is typical of the practical Columba that he added the promise to make 3,000 converts in recompense for the 3,000 dead.

With twelve companions he set sail in a curragh and crossed to the island of Iona where they settled and eventually built a monastery. Columba fulfilled his vow by converting first the islanders and then the Picts of the Scottish mainland. By training and sending out missionaries he spread the message even further afield.

He was boundlessly energetic, building, working in the fields with the monks, striding about the island, crossing to the mainland in a coracle and walking miles over rough country to preach and visit the sick. Many miracles were ascribed to him, including the driving away of a monster in the River Ness by making the sign of the Cross. Could this have been the ancestor of our Loch Ness monster? Once he cared for an injured crane that had been blown off course, and when it was well again and flew away towards Ireland he longed to follow it. However he kept his vow never to see his homeland again — technically at least. It seems that when the bards of Tara appealed to him to come over and settle a dispute, he did so — blindfolded! The saint was loved by everyone who met him, even the animals. When he knew that he would soon die, he blessed the island and promised that it would always be free from snakes. That evening as he sat wearily by a stone cross, the old white horse that carried the milk pails laid its head on his arm and whinnied in distress. Next day, 9th June 597, he died, radiantly happy.

One of the monks trained at Columba's monastery on Iona was Irish-born St Aidan. "A man of remarkable gentleness, goodness and moderation, zealous for God," says Bede. St Aidan's predecessor as missionary to Northumbria, soon discovered that zeal alone was not enough. He was so completely lacking in understanding and gentleness that he alienated people instead of converting them, and the king, St Oswald, asked for someone else to be sent instead. St Aidan was chosen and at once began making converts. In 634 he was appointed bishop and set up his headquarters on Lindisfarne — Holy Island.

The foundations of Christianity in Northumbria had already been laid by St Paulinus, originally sent from Rome to help St Augustine in the south of England. When Princess Ethelburga of Kent married King Edwin of Northumbria, Paulinus went north with her as her chaplain. He was made Archbishop of York and on Easter Day 627 baptised King Edwin and most of his court. After the king was killed in battle by the Mercians, Paulinus brought the widowed queen and her children back to Kent and was later appointed bishop of Rochester.

St Aidan, aided by King Oswald and later by his equally helpful successor King Oswin, continued the good work of St Paulinus, founding churches, monasteries and a school for priests. Two of the pupils there were St Chad, later bishop of Lichfield, and his brother St Cedd who founded the abbey of Lastingham. St Aidan was loved for his unfailing generosity and kindness and because he always practised what he preached. He died at Bamburgh on 31st August 651, and can be recognised in art by his emblem of a stag.

St Oswald was converted to Christianity while an exile on Iona after his father's death. When he regained the throne by defeating the Welsh king, Cadwallon of Gwynedd, he asked the abbot of Iona to send a missionary to Northumbria, and the second one chosen, St Aidan, became a close friend of the King. Oswald had studied Irish while at the monastery, and as it took Aidan some time to master the English tongue, the young king acted as his interpreter. Unfortunately Oswald was killed by Penda, pagan king of Mercia, at the battle of Maserfield (probably Oswestry). His head and hands were cut off and put on stakes, but later found and preserved as relics, the hands at Bamburgh and the head in St Cuthbert's shrine at Durham. St Cuthbert is sometimes portrayed carrying St Oswald's crowned head.

Instead of coming from Ireland, like so many of his predecessors, or from Rome like Paulinus, St Cuthbert was Northumbrian born and bred. While a shepherd boy on the Northumbrian hills he had a vision of St Aidan being carried up to Heaven by angels, and this prompted him to become a monk at Melrose Abbey. In 664 he went with the prior, St Eata, to Lindisfarne, where he became known as a tremendously hard worker, walking miles to preach and visit the sick, but he really preferred to be alone with God and nature and in 676 he withdrew to the little islet of Inner Farne where his only companions were the birds. Eider ducks, of which he was particularly fond, are still known as St Cuthbert's ducks. Eight years later he was summoned from his peaceful hermit's existence to be bishop of Lindisfarne. Although he had now gone up in the world, Bede tells us "he continued to be the same man that he was before," never sparing himself, travelling on foot or horseback to visit all his scattered flock, especially those sick with the plague. He was very knowledgeable about wild animals and anxious to protect them — the first conservationist. Bede, who could be sharply critical at times, had great admiration for him and constantly refers to him as 'the child of God.'

In 687, believing that his death was imminent, Cuthbert retired again to his solitary home on Farne. Some weeks later the abbot and a group of monks from Lindisfarne visited him and stayed with him until he died. It was a dark night and they signalled the news to Lindisfarne by waving torches. Cuthbert would have preferred to be buried on his own little island but prior to his death the monks persuaded him to agree to burial in the church at Lindisfarne. The saint had foreseen the Viking raids which, some 200 years later, forced the monks to flee with his body (still miraculously preserved) first to Chester-le-Street and then to Ripon. Finally his relics were interred in the new cathedral at Durham in 1104.

The Venerable Bede, the historian who gives us so much valuable information about the early Church of England, was born in Northumbria in 673 and died at Jarrow-on-Tyne in 735. He became a monk when very young and spent his whole life studying and writing. His *History of the English Church and People* brought together all available information from a variety of sources and is a masterpiece, although he sometimes let his prejudices show. Because he favoured the Roman as opposed to the Celtic liturgical usage, he approved of

Ninian who was 'regularly instructed at Rome,' but although he wrote with admiration about Aidan's character, he added regretfully, 'but not according to knowledge.'

The differences between the Roman and Celtic customs caused more strife than they would now seem to have warranted. They ranged from the tonsure (Celts had a shaven strip from forehead to crown, Romans shaved the top of the head leaving a fringe all round) to the date of Easter. After the reform of the Roman calendar in 455, one group of Christians would have reached the end of Lent while the others were still at Palm Sunday. In 664 a conference was held at Whitby and victory gained by the Romans, largely because of the influence of St Wilfrid who, although educated at Lindisfarne, had spent some years at Rome and was convinced that the ways of the Roman Church were best.

St Columba's monastery at Iona was the first link in a long chain of Christian education. For instance, St Aidan, trained at Iona, founded a monastery at Lindisfarne; St Wilfrid of York, educated at Lindisfarne founded a monastery at Ripon; St Willibrord, trained at Ripon, became archbishop of Utrecht and founded a monastery at Echternach; and so on.

On the day when he first set covetous eyes on Bishop Finnian's Psalter, St Columba could never have dreamed of the far-reaching consequences.

CHAPTER 6
Celtic Saints

Leprechauns, Cornish piskies, King Arthur and his knights, love philtres, giants and monsters, fairy rings and dancing stones — Celts dearly loved a bit of magic and romance. No wonder the 'lives' of their saints often sound like pure legend. They were not written down for several hundred years, and in the meantime got so entangled and embroidered that it is almost impossible to sift fact from fiction. Better to enjoy them as a whole, remembering that they have a grain of truth and are about real people.

Christianity survived in the Celtic west when the rest of England was invaded by heathen Saxons. Then Augustine brought Rome's form of worship to the south-east. To the Celts the differences, though slight, (mainly the type of tonsure and the date of Easter) were important because they belonged to a form of religion imposed from abroad with its system of bishops, archbishops and, over all, the pope. They wanted to be independent and clung to their monastic system. Augustine's missionaries got no further than Dartmoor and the Severn.

In the 6th century there was a constant coming and going of holy men between Ireland, Wales, Cornwall and Brittany. Cornwall, being a sort of staging post, was well blessed with saints. There are dozens of villages named after them, not only those beginning with 'St' but also some that have no prefix, like Perranzabuloe (Piran-in-the-sands) and Padstow (Petroc's-stow), and others starting with Lan which, like the Welsh Llan, means a monastic enclosure — Landulph, Lanhydrock. Wherever they settled these 'saints' built a cluster of beehive huts and a mud-and-wattle church. They were not canonised and their 'monasteries' were not what we understand by the word today, but they kept Christianity alive.

Chief of the Cornish saints, honoured also in Wales and Brittany was St Petroc, a Welsh prince who supposedly went to Ireland with sixty of his nobles to train as monks. At the end of twenty years they returned to the beach where they had left their boat, and found it miraculously undamaged by wind and tide. Knowing nothing about navigation, they hoisted the sails and set out to wherever God's wind would take them. They were carried safely to Cornwall, coming ashore at the Camel estuary. In the fields nearby they met some reapers. Petroc stopped to pass the time of day and ask what religion they were but, hot and thirsty, they brusquely suggested that a drink of fresh water would be more welcome than a theological discussion. Petroc struck a rock with his staff, and up bubbled a spring of pure cold water, which silenced the scoffing reapers.

The travellers met the hermit saint, Samson, and a friendly bishop, St Wethnoc, who obligingly gave up his cell to St Petroc. The saint and his disciples settled down to a life of strict asceticism. After thirty years (time in these stories is usually given in round figures) he went on pilgrimage to Rome and Jerusalem; one legend claims that he sailed in a silver bowl. Then he moved further east and lived in the wilderness for seven years, existing on a single fish which from time to time was set before him by angelic hands.

On his return to Cornwall, he tamed a horrible monster which had made a habit of gobbling up men and cattle, and removed a splinter from the eye of a dragon that came to him for help. One day a stag fled to him for protection as it was being pursued by Constantine, a wealthy landowner, with his huntsmen and dogs. Petroc forebade anyone to touch the creature. Constantine drew his sword and would have run him through, but he was suddenly seized with paralysis. Petroc cured him, and Constantine and all his followers who had witnessed the scene were instantly converted.

Among the many miracles ascribed to the saint are two with a homely touch. Once when praying out of doors he was caught in a heavy shower, but the rain fell all around without a drop splashing him. On another occasion he and Bishop Wethnoc were sitting talking of holy things when a cloak of dazzling beauty descended from the sky and hovered between them. Each modestly said that the divine gift was intended for the other, and while they were arguing, it sailed up out of sight. A moment later down floated two beautiful cloaks, one for each of them.

The real St Petroc was probably a Welsh prince of the house of Gwent. It seems unlikely that he went to Ireland, but he certainly lived in Cornwall. His monastery at Padstow (Petroc's-stow) was one of the largest in the south west. It became well known as a place of sanctuary for men fleeing from the law, and the town acquired a reputation as a nest of evil-doers which lasted until the right of sanctuary was lost at the Reformation. St Petroc was buried there, but later, when Danes were raiding the coast, his body was moved to the priory at Bodmin, together with his staff and bell.

In 963 King Edgar had a gilded shrine made for St Petroc's bones. Years afterwards the canons went in person to appeal to King Henry I against an unjust tax, taking the shrine with them. On the return journey, they spent the night on Dartmoor, and while they were asleep their horses trespassed into a cornfield. The local peasants, incensed at the damage, attacked the canons, who made a hasty getaway, hidden in a cloud of smoke that issued from the shrine.

In 1176 a disgruntled canon called Martin stole the bones (by this time the gilt casket seems to have disappeared) and took them to the abbey of St Meen in Brittany. A successful appeal for intervention was made to the king, Henry II. As Walter de Coutances, the Lord Privy Seal, was setting out with the letter ordering the monks of St Meen to return the relics, he met a cripple in the street trying to sell a beautiful ivory casket. He bought it on the spot, had an outer wooden box made to protect it, went over to Brittany, collected the relics, placed them in the casket and returned in triumph. This priceless casket, lost for many years, was found in the 18th century in a room over the south porch of Bodmin parish church. In 1957 it was placed in a special glass-fronted niche in the wall of the south aisle, where it may still be seen.

Next to St Petroc in importance is St Piran, patron saint of tin-miners and actually credited in one story with the discovery of tin in

Cornwall. Medieval monks trying to write about him, but unable to find any authentic details, borrowed from the 'life' of an Irish saint with a somewhat similar name, St Ciaran.

According to this, he began life with a good omen; shortly before his birth, his mother dreamed that a star had fallen into her mouth. As a young man St Piran studied at Rome, and while travelling in Italy, met St Patrick who gave him a bell and told him to return to Ireland and build a monastery on the spot where the bell would ring out clearly of its own accord. St Piran obeyed the instructions, his first 'monastery' being a humble cell and his first 'monks' a fox, a badger, a wolf and a doe.

The miracles ascribed to him, as to many of the Celtic saints, fall mainly into two categories — the classical legendary type (slaying or taming monsters) and the Biblical type (healing or even raising from the dead). A few, however, are of an endearing practical nature. When a mischievous youth extinguished the monastery fire causing a visiting saint to complain of the cold, a ball of fire descended from heaven at St Piran's request and warmed the chilly saint.

St Piran's arrival in Cornwall was more dramatic than that of St Petroc. A group of Irish pagans attacked him, tied him to a millstone and rolled it over the edge of a cliff into the stormy sea. The waves subsided and the unorthodox craft floated safely to the Cornish coast, drifting ashore near Newquay. Here the saint built a little church among the shifting sand-dunes. It was gradually engulfed by wind-blown sand, and by the 12th century was completely buried. A replacement, built a few miles away, had to be abandoned in its turn and early in the 19th century yet another church was built. Soon afterwards the shifting dunes revealed a tiny church, only 26 feet long, perfectly preserved by the sand in which it had lain buried for at least 800 years. It is popularly believed to be the church built by St Piran himself, and even the experts admit that it must have been built about the right time. It was carefully excavated and a protective shell built round it — not very beautiful, but a practical way of preserving for posterity this vivid reminder of the saint. However far-fetched are the stories about him, there can be little doubt that he really did live nearby.

Welsh ruling families at this time were enthusiastic monastery-founders and a number of Celtic saints are claimed to have been Welsh princes, or at least 'of noble blood', and to have belonged to one of these 'houses'. The most important monastery, at Llancarfan near Cardiff, was founded by St Cadoc who gave his name to many places in Wales and is also honoured in Cornwall and Brittany. He is supposed to have made missionary journeys all over Europe, and ten pilgrimages, three to Jerusalem and seven to Rome. His most spectacular journey was his last when he was transported on a cloud to Benevento in Italy to be made a bishop. Soon afterwards he was martyred while celebrating Mass.

A Llancarfan monk whose name is well-known today because of the Breton port near which he lived, is St Malo, who spent most of his working life in Brittany. A charming story tells how one warm day while working in a vineyard he took off his hood and hung it on a branch. When he came back he found some wrens had made a nest in it and, rather than disturb them, he managed without it until the wren family had been safely reared.

St Samson also came from Wales and settled in Brittany, having spent some time as a hermit in Cornwall where he met St Petroc. In his early days he survived an attempt by jealous fellow-monks to poison him. The monastery cat died after tasting the herbal liquid which Samson drank without coming to any harm.

When St Carantoc left his native Wales for south-west England, he trusted to divine providence to decide where he should settle. Throwing his portable altar into the Bristol Channel, he said that he would build a church wherever it came ashore. He lost sight of it on the way, and it was found by King Arthur who fancied using it as a table. However, anything that was put on it either slid to the ground or was thrown far away by unseen hands. Carantoc arrived looking for his altar and, having convinced the king of his holiness by ridding the district of a monstrous serpent, was given not only his altar but also a generous piece of land to settle on.

Although the logical step from Wales to Brittany was by way of Cornwall, most of these travelling saints are said to have visited Ireland as well, even if the time they are supposed to have spent there would make them centenarians before they could possibly have completed all their adventures! This is because before their 'lives' were written, some six or seven hundred years later, Ireland had become the training ground *par excellence*, and all biographers felt obliged to include a period of study there for their heroes.

The biographers of St Budoc found an unusual slant to his story. St Budoc may, like so many others, have gone to Brittany from Wales, but his 'life' claims that he was of a noble Breton family. His mother, St Azenor, was falsely accused of infidelity. In a fit of rage her husband put her in a barrel and cast it into the sea. While it drifted towards Ireland, St Azenor gave birth to a son. Mother and child were washed ashore near Waterford and rescued by monks from the nearby monastery who adopted the baby, calling him Beuzec, meaning drowned, because he came from the sea.

Years later Azenor's husband learned the truth. Bitterly regretting his lack of trust, he went in search of her and eventually found her and the son he had never seen. He planned to take them back to Brittany, but before he could arrange this, first he and then Azenor died. Beuzec, now a monk, made up his mind to go alone. He was too impatient to wait for a ship, and made the crossing in a stone coffin! Legend now catches up with fact. St Budoc really did become bishop of Dol in Brittany, where he died in 500 AD. His relics are preserved in a silver reliquary in the church at Plourin, and it is said that anyone swearing falsely on them will be punished in a year and a day.

St Budoc sent groups of missionary monks across the sea from Brittany to south-west England. In their fragile open boats they sailed into the estuaries of the Fal and Tamar and established their settlements there. The Tamar one was on 'Budock's-hide' (Budock's piece of land), now known as Budshead, and the neighbouring district of Plymouth is called St Budeaux.

In Cornwall he gave his name to Budoc Vean and Budock Water as well as St Budock's church in Falmouth. Cornwall's St Budock, Brittany's St Beuzec and Plymouth's St Budeaux was known in Dyfed, west Wales, where he may have been born, as St Buddock and even St Buttock. A small chapel in the grounds of the old priory near Milford Haven was known as St Buttock's, and the name was passed on to the big house later built on the site. However a subsequent owner felt this was rather indelicate and changed the name to St Botolph's.

Not far from St Budoc's settlement at Falmouth is St Mawes — St Maudet's. He is said to have lived for many years on a small island two miles off the coast of Brittany. It was infested with snakes until he banished them and this gave him the reputation of being able to cure 'worms.' Sufferers would stir a spoonful of soil from the island into water and drink it in the hope of a cure.

In spite of the strong association between Cornish and Breton saints, St Ives, on the north Cornish coast, has nothing to do with the Breton lawyer-saint, Yves. The patron of St Ives is Ia, a female Irish saint who literally missed the boat when, with some missionary companions, she was on the point of setting out for Cornwall. Finding that they had gone without her, she stepped on a leaf and sailed across on that instead. The number of stories of saints travelling in unlikely craft is probably due to the fact that their boats, coracles and curraghs, looked so unseaworthy. No wonder that a saint's first act on stepping safely ashore was to build an oratory to give thanks!

St Cuby, another inveterate traveller, appears to be the only Cornish saint born in Cornwall. He was the son of St Selevan, sometimes called St Levan. During his obligatory stay in Ireland, he had a long feud with a neighbour named Fintam, mainly about land. St Cuby's frail elderly cousin had to keep to a milk diet, so the saint gave him a cow and calf. One day the calf strayed on to Fintam's land. He found it, tied it to a tree, and absolutely refused to return it. St Cuby prayed for the calf to come back. It did — dragging the tree with it, roots and all.

When the saint decided to sail with some companions to Wales, they set about making a coracle. They had completed the wicker frame but not yet covered it with hides, when Fintam turned up and taunted them by saying that if their faith was really strong they would sail in it as it was. The saint accepted the challenge and they set off at once, running almost immediately into a violent storm. In spite of this they arrived safely at Holyhead on the island of Anglesey, called in Welsh, *Caergybi*, after St Cuby.

One day while the local king was hunting, his dog chased a nanny-goat which ran to St Cuby for protection. The saint asked for, and was granted, all the land encircled by the dog and goat in their chase. On this land he founded the famous monastery in which he eventually died.

Several saints are a type of package deal, including St Neot who is a confusion of two saints, one Saxon, one Celtic, with two sets of legends. The Saxon tradition claims that he was King Alfred's friend and adviser, perhaps even his elder brother who renounced the throne to become a monk. The Celtic tradition is naturally richer in legends. One says that when he found his parishioners were staying away from church because they had to scare the crows from their fields, the saint sent for the birds and told them that on Sundays they must confine their activities to one particular field — which to this day is called Crowpound.

One of the beautiful stained glass windows in St Neot's tiny church depicts scenes from his life. One shows him using four stags to draw his plough as someone had stolen his oxen; the thief was so impressed at this sight that he not only returned the oxen but became a monk himself.

St Neot had a habit of sitting with his feet in his holy well while he read the psalter. Some say that he immersed himself up to the neck, which would be all too easy if there is any truth in another story, that he was only fifteen inches tall! In the church window, however, he is shown with his feet in a tub, looking like someone trying to ward off a cold by soaking them in a mustard bath.

Rather like St Petroc and his everlasting fish, St Neot was promised that three fish in the well would provide him with food for ever on condition that he never ate more than one at a time. One day he fell ill and his servant, convinced that he was not getting enough to eat, caught and prepared two of the fish. The saint ordered him to throw the extra one back in the well, and although it had been well cooked, it swam away quite happily.

St Mylor or Melor, popular in Brittany and patron of two Cornish parishes and of Amesbury in Wiltshire, was a long-suffering little boy. When he was seven years old, his father was killed by his wicked uncle

Rivoldus, who considered killing the child too, but settled for cutting off his right hand and left foot and confining him in a monastery. Well-wishers made the little saint a silver hand and brazen foot which, miraculously, grew with him. He was a pious, unambitious child, but Rivoldus feared his increasing popularity and bribed his guardian with rich lands in exchange for the boy's head. The murder did neither of them any good, for Rivoldus went mad and died in torment, and while the guardian was surveying his new lands from a hilltop, his eyes fell out and he too died a horrible death. Meanwhile the boy's body had been put on an ox-cart. The beasts stubbornly refused to go the way the drivers wanted, but insisted on going to a particular spot at which point the cart became quite immovable. This was taken as a divine sign, and the body buried there.

St Keyne was a female saint who could turn adders into stones and whose well had one peculiar property. Whichever partner in a marriage drank the water first would gain mastery over the household. Robert Southey describes in an amusing poem how a bridegroom left his new wife at the church porch to dash to the well, but she had forestalled him by taking a bottle of the water into church for the ceremony!

It is said that during the 6th century there were more saints in Cornwall than in heaven!

CHAPTER 7

Crusader and Cathedral Saints

By the 11th century the West had become Christian. Pilgrims flocked to the holy shrines and all who possibly could made the long journey to the most sacred shrine of all, the Holy Sepulchre in Jerusalem. Towards the end of the century, however, the Holy Land was overrun by Muslim Turks. The struggle to rescue it from the infidel went on for over 200 years and caused the death of millions of people.

The First Crusade was brought about largely because a pope, Urban II, found himself temporarily redundant. His predecessor, Gregory VII, had quarrelled with and ultimately excommunicated the German emperor, Henry IV, who retaliated by appointing a Pope of his own. This 'anti-Pope', Guibert, was in possession when Urban was officially appointed in 1088. Urban bent his energies instead to realising a dream, the reconquest of the Holy Land.

French-born and a former monk of the famous monastery at Cluny, Urban went to France to begin putting his plan into practice by calling a council at Clermont and urging the need for a Holy War. Even he was astonished at the result. Powerful princes of the West flocked with their armies to 'take the Cross', assembling in Constantinople between the summer of 1096 and the following spring. There was also an even more fervent army of peasants who, knowing no world beyond their own little hamlets, blindly followed Peter the Hermit.

With jealousy, desertion and betrayal on both sides, the Holy War was not all that holy, but at least Antioch, Edessa, Tripoli and eventually Jerusalem itself were regained. Godfrey of Bouillon became king of Jerusalem and crusader states with their own rulers were centred on the other three towns. Pilgrims once more visited the Holy Land and Italian merchants settled at the ports.

Then in 1144 Edessa was again lost to the Muslims, and St Bernard of Clairvaux inspired Louis VII of France and Conrad III of Germany to lead the Second, disastrous, Crusade. In 1187 the Muslim leader, Saladin, recaptured Jerusalem; this led to the Third Crusade when the rulers of Europe — Richard the Lionheart of England, Frederick Barbarossa of Germany, and Philip Augustus of France — united, after a fashion, in a gruelling campaign. They captured Acre but failed to regain Jerusalem.

The fourth Crusade, engineered by the Venetians, was directed against Constantinople and resulted in such an appalling massacre that the pope excommunicated the crusaders. Then came the courageous but pathetic Children's Crusade, inspired by a boy in the Vendome region; youngsters poured enthusiastically into the ports of France and Italy, trusting that God would find them a way over the sea to the Holy Land, but that was not how things worked out.

In 1229 Emperor Frederick, by some cunning negotiation, regained Jerusalem from the Muslims. This was rather frowned upon by some who thought that it ought to have been won in glorious battle. In any case less than two decades later the Muslims were in possession again, inspiring France's saintly king, Louis IX, to lead yet another crusade.

The most obvious effect of these long drawn out wars was the drain on manpower and resources. Among other far-reaching results was the growth of the Orders of Knights. The Templars, distinguished by a red cross on their white tunics, were originally a type of police force quartered near the temple in Jerusalem. Later they became immensely rich and powerful, witness their fortresses on Mediterranean shores. The Hospitallers, Knights of the Order of St John of Jerusalem, ran a hospital in the city; on their black gowns they wore the white cross which is still the badge of the St John ambulance brigade.

Anyone who took the Cross was granted absolution from his sins and dying on a crusade was thought to be a certain way to salvation. Later simply going on a pilgrimage was considered enough. Corrupt clergy made a scandalous living out of the indiscriminate sale of par-

A Knight Hospitaller.

dons, indulgences and bogus relics. A great many relics, genuine or not, were brought back by the crusaders, together with the cult of eastern saints, especially St George who, they claimed, lent them miraculous aid at the siege of Acre.

The two saints most directly associated with the Crusades were Bernard of Clairvaux and Louis IX of France. St Bernard was born at Fontaines near Dijon in 1090. His family were well-to-do and he had a happy childhood, although he was delicate and stayed at home to be taught by his mother while his five brothers went off to school. He finished his education in a school at Chatillon-sur-Seine and proved as brilliant as his clever brothers. However he was not strong enough to follow them into the army and at nineteen returned home. His mother's death resolved his intention to become a monk.

The monastery of Cîteaux was one of the few that still adhered to the strict rule of St Benedict. The monks were all getting on in years and the monastery sadly needed some new young blood. It was saved by St Bernard who not only joined it himself but brought along four of his brothers and twenty-five friends.

Two years later Bernard was ordered by the pope to leave the now revitalised monastery at Cîteaux and, taking twelve monks with him, to found a new one at Aube in Champagne. It was a wild, robber-infested valley, but they worked hard at clearing and planting the land and made it so fertile that Bernard renamed it Clairvaux — Valley of Light. Cistercians, the White Monks, have always retained their interest in agriculture. The rule was a hard one; sometimes it had to be relaxed if a monk was in danger of dying of overwork and starvation — but they were a happy community and the monastery prospered so well that it became the mother house to sixty-eight other Cistercian establishments.

St Bernard remained a shy, modest man, but because of his wisdom and sense of justice he was frequently asked to give advice and to intervene in disputes. In spite of his gentleness, he could be severely critical when necessary, and made many enemies by speaking out frankly against the luxurious life-style of some of the clergy.

The pope sent him to preach against the Albigensian heresy in southern France. In this he was so successful that he became known as 'the scourge of the heretics,' and he brought about the downfall of the philosopher Peter Abelard.

When Edessa fell to the Muslims in 1144, Bernard was given a task for which he was well suited, preaching the Second Crusade. He travelled throughout France and Germany, and his eloquence brought an enthusiastic response not only from the pious king of France, Louis VII, but even from the German emperor Conrad III, which the saint regarded as a miracle. It was all in vain, however, for the Crusade was a dismal failure and St Bernard was widely blamed for having inspired it.

He was the embodiment of all that was best in his century, and his sermons and writings were so outstanding that he was declared a Doctor of the Church in 1830. Like St Ambrose, the other 'honey-sweet doctor,' St Bernard has a beehive as his emblem.

The saint most closely associated with the Crusades was Louis IX of France, St Louis. He was such a model ruler that 500 years later Voltaire, no lover of kings, said, "It was hardly possible for any man to reach such great excellence."

In 1226, a few months after the death of St Francis of Assisi, Louis VIII died very suddenly of a fever, and his twelve-year old son found himself king of a troubled country. Under the wise guidance of the regent, his mother, Queen Blanche, the boy king managed to keep in order his powerful, quarrelsome barons. He would have much preferred to be a monk, but he carried out his kingly duties with wisdom and compassion, always making a point of travelling to meet as many of the ordinary people as he could, being accessible to everybody, and administering justice impartially and kindly.

At the age of fifteen he married Margaret of Provence, whose younger sister, Eleanor, was the wife of Henry III of England. Louis defeated Henry's army in battles at Taillebourg and at Saintes, but his generous terms and the family association eased tension between the two countries.

Baldwin of Constantinople visited France several times pleading for help against the Muslims. Louis bought from him an extremely precious relic, the Crown of Thorns, and built the beautiful Sainte-Chapelle in Paris to enshrine it.

In 1244 Louis nearly died of fever and his recovery made him determined to take the Cross. The sultan of Damascus had allowed Christians to re-occupy Jerusalem, but now the sultan of Egypt drove them out again. Louis was bent on leading another crusade to regain the Holy City. After four years he assembled his army of 7,000 at Aigues-Mortes in the south of France. Accompanied by his wife and his impetuous, quarrelsome brothers, he embarked in August, 1248.

As it was the Egyptian ruler who was to blame for the plight of the Christians, Louis began his campaign by landing in Egypt and attacking Damietta. He won an easy victory, but afterwards the troops, unused to the intense heat of an Egyptian summer, became lazy and undisciplined. Louis was persuaded by his brother, the Comte d'Artois, to engage in another battle at Mansurah. It was a hard-won, empty victory for the French and the young count was killed. Instead of retreating to Damietta, Louis allowed his lines of supply to be cut off. Too late he tried to break through to his base, but his troops were routed and the king was taken prisoner. In captivity he showed extraordinary fortitude. His courage and patience were an example to his fellow-prisoners, and he helped to care for the sick and injured.

At last the ransom money was raised. The king was released and went to Acre, where Margaret, who had been left behind at Damietta, rejoined him with their newborn son. Louis was determined to stay in Palestine — the historian Joinville advised him that as the Muslim leaders were quarrelling among themselves, there might be a chance of seizing Jerusalem — but his brothers and most of the barons returned home. He stayed there four years, rebuilding defences (often with his own hands) and winning many converts. He was short of men and money and it was only the supplies his mother was able to send from France that kept him going. When she died, he and his wife and children returned home, and he set about being a moral ruler, noted for his unostentatious piety. It is said that he wore shoes without soles as he did not want to make a show of walking barefoot. Even the humblest of his subjects was free to approach him while he sat under an oak tree in the Bois de Vincennes. Visiting scholars were always sure of a welcome and he encouraged learning in every possible way. He was more cut out to be a stay-at-home ruler than a conquering hero, but unfortunately he felt obliged to take the Cross again. In July, 1270, he set out once more, this time leaving his wife behind, but taking three of their eleven children. They crossed to North Africa but Louis was soon taken ill and died at Tunis on the 25th August. His son Philip brought his body back to Paris where it was buried in the Abbey of St Denis.

One of the things that Louis absolutely forebade was the use of bad language. He never swore, and would not allow anyone else to do so in front of him. The same is said of France's other warrior saint, Joan of Arc, but apart from their piety they had little else in common. The king's heart never seemed to be in the fight; he disliked bloodshed, and at home in France gave up hunting and made duelling illegal. He embarked on his crusades only from a strong sense of duty and seems to have had little military acumen. St Joan, on the other hand, although she undertook her campaign at the instigation of her 'voices', gloried in her certainty that she was carrying out God's command and driving the enemy from her beloved country.

It is often said that young people today grow up too quickly. By the age of nineteen, Joan had led troops to victory, been wounded in battle, caused a king to be crowned, and endured harsh imprisonment and a cruel death.

She was born in 1412 (almost 200 years after St Louis) at Domrèmy on the Meuse, daughter of Jacques Darc. Except for her extreme piety she was a typical, illiterate, hardworking, friendly, peasant child. What set her apart from the others was the fact that from the age of thirteen she claimed she heard the voices of three saints — St Michael, St Catherine of Alexandria and St Margaret of Antioch — instructing her how to behave.

At that time France was at war with Burgundy and England, whose forces occupied almost all the northern part of the country. Henry VI of England claimed the French throne, technically vacant for five years as the dauphin had never been crowned. Prompted by her voices and after much persistence, Joan managed to obtain an audience with the dauphin at Chinon. To test her he hid himself among his courtiers when she was ushered into his presence, but she spotted him at once.

So persuasive was she that she was eventually given her own standard and allowed to join the troops at Blois, whence she led them to a convincing victory at Orléans. The English were routed and the wavering dauphin was so impressed that he allowed himself to be bullied and coaxed by her into being crowned at Rheims in July, 1429, as King Charles VII.

She inspired such enthusiasm and confidence in her troops that they had a series of successes, but she never realised her dream of entering Paris in triumph, for things went wrong at Compiègne. She was captured by the Burgundians and sold to the English. Accused of blasphemy because she claimed divine inspiration, she endured harsh imprisonment and a farcical trial. Eventually she was burn at the stake in the market-place at Rouen, begging the monk who was with her to shout his words of comfort louder than the crackling of the fire, and to hold the crucifix high so that it would be the last thing she saw. There has never been anyone else quite like St Joan. She saved France at a crucial stage in the Hundred Years War and changed the course of history.

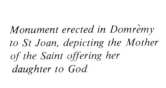

Monument erected in Domrèmy to St Joan, depicting the Mother of the Saint offering her daughter to God

Another young woman who had a considerable influence on international affairs in spite of coming from a modest background, was St Catherine of Siena. Born about 1347, Catherine Benincasa was the twenty-fifth child of a Sienese dyer. Her mother was short-tempered and sharp-tongued — not surprising with so many children — and must have looked forward to getting the last of the large brood off her hands. Catherine, however, like the virgin martyrs of Roman times, decided that she wanted to devote her life to God and marriage was not for her, although as she was extremely pretty there were plenty of suitors. To make herself less attractive, she cut off her beautiful hair. Her mother was furious and even her more easy-going father decided that she must be punished. She was made to do the servant's work, but this was no hardship for her as she was happiest when performing menial tasks. Eventually they relented and allowed her to become a tertiary sister of the Dominican Order, working among the sick and poor and even nursing people dying of the plague. When not working she spent her time meditating and had many wonderful spiritual experiences. She became well known in Siena and a 'Catherine group,' the Caterinati, gathered round her and stayed with her when she travelled abroad.

In 1305, Pope Clement V, a Frenchman, moved the papal residence to Avignon in France. He was followed by several other French popes of whom the last (excluding the anti-popes) was Gregory XI. He was pope in Catherine's time and she was convinced that if he would return to Rome his presence would have a unifying effect on the divided country. So she travelled to Avignon and, in spite of French opposition, persuaded the hesitant pope that it was his duty to return to Rome. This had the desired effect for a time, but after Gregory's death in 1378 his successor, Urban VI, ran into trouble again and for forty years the western church was divided by the 'great schism'.

Catherine was famed for her wisdom and her advice was sought by those in authority — she even negotiated treaties — but above all she was loved and honoured for her holiness. Although she never learnt to write, she dictated a mass of letters to important people and her book, '*Dialogue,*' was a great theological work. She is one of Italy's patron saints (with St Francis) and in 1970 was declared a Doctor of the Church.

Medieval Christendom had its ups and downs but its great glory was the building of magnificent cathedrals like Chartres, Rheims, Rouen, Strasbourg, Canterbury, Salisbury, Lincoln and Wells. All over Europe towers and spires soared towards the sky, symbols of men's heavenly aspirations. Inside, too, the eye was carried upwards by high vaulted roofs and pointed arches. Richly-coloured stained glass windows provided a pictorial Bible for those who could not read, and the carvings in wood and stone were as good as a sermon. Souls writhing in torment, gleeful devils and loathesome monsters were a dreadful warning to sinners. The fear of hell was vivid and ever-present, as was the hope of reward in heaven. Statues of saints helped to concentrate devotion; they were usually distinguished by their special 'attributes' so that the right one could be invoked for any particular request.

Every cathedral has a close association with at least one saint — someone who lived and worked there or died on the spot (perhaps violently) or whose relics it enshrines. The saint may have actually been buried in the cathedral, or his relics transported from somewhere else — not always legitimately.

Canterbury numbers at least eight saints among its archbishops. The first archbishop was St Augustine who, sent by Pope Gregory, landed with his forty Benedictine monks at Ebbsfleet in Kent in 597. They were well received by the local king, a tolerant man whose French wife was already a Christian. He not only allowed them to preach, but after a while was baptised himself and encouraged his subjects to follow suit. He gave them land to build an abbey and helped to rebuild the ruined Roman church which was to become the first Canterbury cathedral. From here Christianity spread all over southern England, and northwards to converge with the Northumbrian missionaries.

In 667 AD the newly appointed archbishop died before he could take up office and, to everyone's surprise, the pope chose instead a sixty-six year old Greek monk from Tarsus, St Theodore. He turned out to be an excellent choice, a remarkable scholar who made Canterbury an important centre of learning and an able administrator who laid down the framework of diocesan organisation which still exists.

Nearly three hundred years later St Odo the Good, son of a Danish chieftain, became archbishop. The cathedral was in a shocking state of disrepair and the roof so leaky that Odo had to have it removed completely. For three whole years while repairs were being carried out, not one drop of rain fell on the building, or so the story goes. As Odo is reputed to have been an extremely eloquent preacher, perhaps his congregation were too entranced by his sermons to notice if they were being rained on!

Odo's successor, St Dunstan, born at Glastonbury in about 910, was the first great churchman-statesman, the friend and adviser of four kings of Wessex. He was brought up at court and sent abroad to be trained as a Benedictine monk. On his return he made his home in a tiny cell in a churchyard where he fasted until he began to have hallucinations. One day when he was working at his forge the devil came to tempt him and would not leave him alone until the saint seized his nose with his red-hot pincers. This is why St Dunstan is often shown holding tongs.

Handsome and charming, he seems to have been good at everything, not only book learning but practical things like music, painting, poetry, metalwork and jewellery-making. Despite his many accomplishments he was modest and likeable. He practised strict self-discipline according to the Benedictine Rule and expected his monks to do the same. Even St Dunstan could not entirely avoid making enemies, and he had a spell of exile under one of the boy kings, Edwy, but for nearly twenty years he ruled the country in all but name. Then after the accession of Ethelred the Unready, he spent more time at Canterbury where he died in 988.

St Alphege, who had been bishop of Winchester for twenty years, became archbishop in 1005 at a time when the country was overrun by Danes. Ethelred had not paid them the promised tribute, and in revenge they sacked Canterbury and took the archbishop prisoner. They offered to exchange him for an extortionate sum, but Alphege refused to be ransomed, knowing what hardship it would cause his people to raise the money. He was dragged around in chains for several months, and finally while his captors were having a drunken carousal at Greenwich, they pelted him with ox-bones, severely injuring him, and finally one of the Danes struck off his head with an axe.

Next day they handed the body over to the people of London who buried it at Old St Paul's, and some years later King Canute, himself a Dane, transferred the relics with great pomp to Canterbury cathedral. There was some doubt about whether St Alphege could strictly be called a martyr, but the next archbishop to be canonised, St Anselm, asserted that he was.

Before St Anselm's time the Saxon cathedral was destroyed by fire. Lanfranc, the wise and energetic archbishop appointed by William the Conqueror, began rebuilding it in 1070. He was an excellent archbishop (one of the few people who could influence the headstrong king) but never made the saintly grade.

The next king, William Rufus, thought that without an archbishop he would be able to keep the church revenues himself, so when Lanfranc died he refused to appoint a successor. Then he fell seriously ill and, fearing death, appointed Anselm, a gentle scholarly monk, whom he thought he could bully. In spite of his quiet nature, however, St Anselm could be very stubborn when he felt the church was threatened, and he stood up to both King William II and his successor, Henry I. Before his death in 1109, St Anselm had several spells of exile, and perhaps for this reason his symbol is a ship.

Canterbury was really put on the map by the next saint, Thomas à Becket. Murdered at his own altar, he was at once recognised as a saint and martyr, and his cathedral became a world-famous place of pilgrimage.

Finally there is St Edmund, scholarly and kind, not very successful as an archbishop, but who always genuinely tried to do what he thought was right. He was born at Abingdon in about 1170 of well-to-do parents. He loved learning and made the most of his education at Oxford and Paris, returning to Oxford to lecture in theology. In 1222 he went to Salisbury to be cathedral treasurer, and in the following year was appointed archbishop of Canterbury. They were troubled times, and St Edmund's piety and scholarship were not enough. He needed a practical administrator, and found one in Richard de Wich (St Richard of Chichester) whom he made his chancellor.

St Edmund made certain necessary reforms and was able to avert a civil war in the Welsh Marches, but he was involved in disputes with the king, Henry III, and with the monks of Canterbury, which hindered him in his work. He was on his way to Rome to plead his cause when he died at Pontigny in France.

The Middle Ages were a time of groping after truth. Dissension was caused sometimes by greed, ambition or fear, more often by a genuine clash of beliefs. In spite of the strife, there were two great manifestations of Christian faith — the crusades and the cathedrals.

The word apathy, so often used in connection with religion (or lack of it) today, could certainly not be applied to Christendom in the Middle Ages.

CHAPTER 8
𝕽𝖊𝖑𝖎𝖌𝖎𝖔𝖚𝖘 𝕺𝖗𝖉𝖊𝖗𝖘

Missionaries spread the faith, martyrs died for it, crusaders defended it in battle but every now and again someone was needed to take a long look at the Christian way of life and reorganise it. This is what St Benedict did.

The idea that it was possible to get close to God only by withdrawing from one's fellow-men was not a new one. From the earliest days of Christianity men had gone to live alone in the wilderness, sometimes fleeing from persecution, more often seeking to achieve perfection of the soul by mortification of the body. Some chose an island (there is still a monastery on the French island of Lérins where Honoratus, influenced by St Anthony Abbot, settled over fifteen hundred years ago) but most went to the deserts of Upper Egypt, Libya and Gaza; gaunt, unwelcoming cliffs where no green thing grew and where a spring of pure water was truly a miracle.

The first of these 'desert fathers' was Paul of Thebes, a refugee from the persecution of Decius. He found such satisfaction in his ascetic, solitary way of life that he never returned to civilisation, and as he lived to well over a hundred he is a good advertisement for it. St Jerome, who himself spent several years living in this manner, wrote about the life of Paul the Hermit. He describes how St Anthony visited the old man and was with him when he died. He wrapped the body in the cloak which his famous friend St Athanasius had given him. As he was struggling to dig a grave in the hard ground, two lions bounded up. Instead of attacking him, they scraped a shallow hole with their claws, and then waited meekly to receive the saint's blessing.

St Anthony also lived to be over a hundred; he was born in 251 and died in 356. During his time as a hermit he was dramatically tempted by the devil, a theme which has proved popular with artists, especially as one of the temptations involved beautiful women! One of the devil's complaints, we are told, was that so many men were following St Anthony's example that the desert, traditional home of demons, was swarming with hermits! Certainly there were a great many of them. St Anthony and another desert father, St Pachomius began organising them into groups. St Pachomius exercised more authority over his hermitages than St Anthony, whose establishments were more individualistic. The hermits lived in caves or cells within reach of each other, but came together occasionally for a communal act of worship. They spent most of their time in prayer, concentrating so much on the state of their souls that they neglected or deliberately mortified their bodies, often fasting almost to the point of death.

The best-known example of extreme self-mortification is St Simeon Stylites. In his efforts to attain absolute purity of heart, he first tried walling himself up in a cave, then chaining himself to a rock, and finally living on top of a pillar. Instead of giving him the seclusion he craved, this strange way of life brought people flocking from all over Europe, first from curiosity and then, as news of his kindness and wisdom spread, to seek his advice. From time to time the height of his pillar was increased until it reached about fifty feet. He lived on top of it for thirty years, hauling up in a basket just enough food to keep himself alive. He was exposed to the elements except when he was ill, when he allowed himself a rough shelter which he removed as soon as he was fit again. His fame meant that he was able to mediate in disputes, and his example of asceticism was widely followed.

St Benedict lived roughly a hundred years after St Simeon and two hundred after St Anthony. By this time there were many monasteries, but the rules by which they were regulated were spasmodic and ineffective. St Benedict's great contribution was to formulate one rule by which all monks should live. It was clear and comprehensive, setting out the daily time-table — six hours were to be spent in prayer, five in manual work (to keep the monastery as self-supporting as possible) and four in reading the Bible and other religious works. The monks were to have no personal possessions, to maintain silence most of the time and to be humble and obedient. The abbot, appointed for life, was to have absolute authority, but he must bear in mind that he would be answerable to God.

The rule demanded discipline, hard work and devotion, but no excessive self-mortification. St Benedict called it a rule for beginners. Although he was very strict with himself, he made allowances for others who had less stamina, physical or moral, even those sleepy-heads who might creep in late for midnight or early morning services. He said that bedding and clothing should be adequate; wine was to be permitted in moderation, and at mealtimes there should be an alternative course in case any monk was unable to eat the one offered. Moderation was the important word in all things; indigestion was unpardonable since it suggested excess!

We know more about St Benedict than about most of his contemporaries because St Gregory described his life in his '*Dialogues*.' His account is embellished with unlikely miracles, but the basic facts are probably correct as St Gregory claims that he got them at first hand from four of St Benedict's own monks.

He was born at Nursia, seventy miles north of Rome, in about 480. His family were well-to-do, staunch Christians. He and his twin sister Scholastica, had a very strict upbringing, so that when, at the age of fourteen, he went to Rome to study, he was shocked by the licentiousness he found there. After a while, with a few other monks, he went to Enfide, about forty miles from Rome. Then deciding that he needed complete solitude, he went alone to Subiaco, where Nero had built his summer palace. He found a mountain-cave overlooking the lake, and settled there to the life of a hermit.

There were other monks living in the area and one of them, Romanus, brought his frugal food, lowering it to him on a rope. With no other distractions, he was unwittingly acquiring a reputation for holiness and when the abbot of a nearby monastery died, the monks asked him to take his place.

He was reluctant to leave his cave, but realising that reforms were badly needed, accepted the post and zealously set about the task. While the more serious-minded members of the community appreciated his reforms, others resented his strictness and there was even an attempt to poison him. One day as he was lifting the chalice to his lips, he made the sign of the cross over it and it shattered, spilling the poison. Because of this incident, his emblem is a broken cup.

Once again St Benedict moved on, this time to Monte Cassino, about halfway between Rome and Naples. It was largely a pagan area, so there was plenty of scope for evangelising. The number of followers grew, and on top of the mountain they founded the monastery which was to become world famous. The original monastery was destroyed during the second world war, but has since been re-built.

For six hundred years St Bendict's rule remained more or less unchallenged, but inevitably there were some who rebelled against its strictness and others for whom it was not strict enough. There were several 'reformed' orders, including the *Carthusians* founded by St Bruno, and the *Cistercians*, founded initially by Robert de Molesme, but firmly estblished by St Bernard. Over the years the tolerance of occasional weakness allowed by St Benedict's rule degenerated into slackness. Part of the trouble was that there were so few careers for educated men that many joined monasteries simply because there was nothing better to do. It was even more difficult for women; unless they could make a good marriage they drifted into convents with no real sense of dedication. Religious establishments became rich, and often greedy, because nobles gave money in the hope of buying a place in heaven. Reformers wanted to return to the rule of St Benedict and apply it even more strictly than he had done himself.

St Bruno, born in Cologne in 1033, was a promising pupil at the cathedral school at Rheims and later returned there as professor of theology, a post he held successfully for twenty years. He was made chancellor of the cathedral, working well with Archbishop Gervase, but when Gervase died, Bruno quarrelled with his successor, an undesirable character called Manasses, and was dismissed.

Bruno had long felt drawn towards a life of contemplation, and now circumstances obliged him to realise his dream. In 1084, with six friends, he went up into the mountains near Grenoble, and built a church and a group of huts that developed into the famous hermitage of La Grande Chartreuse.

The monks conformed to a very strict version of St Benedict's rule, spending their time in prayer and manual labour, eating no meat and wearing hair shirts. Their reputation impressed Pope Urban II, who had once been a pupil of St Bruno's and who was concerned at the general slackness in monasteries. He summoned Bruno to Rome to ask his advice about reforms, and offered to make him an archbishop. Bruno refused and was allowed instead to found another monastery in Calabria on the lines of La Grande Chartreuse. By the time of his death in 1101 the Carthusian order was well established. It continued to prosper and Carthusian monasteries (Charterhouses) spread far afield.

A contemporary of St Bruno was Robert de Molesme. He too was disturbed by the general slackness in monasteries and founded one of his own at Molesme. Still dissatisfied, he took a few monks to Cîteaux, near Dijon, and established another there. After eighteen months he returned to Molesme, being succeeded at Cîteaux first by St Alberic and then by an Englishman, Stephen Harding.

These three men were the official founders of the Cistercian order, but it might well have faded into obscurity if St Bernard, with his four brothers and twenty-five friends, had not arrived to give it a new lease of life. After establishing Cîteaux on a firm footing, St Bernard and some of his companions moved on to found another monastery in the wild valley which they tamed and called Clairvaux, Valley of Light. This land reclamation and development became a feature of the Cistercian Order. They set up monasteries in out-of-the-way places and by hard manual labour became self-supporting.

Cistercians and Carthusians stemmed directly from the Benedictines. Another order formed about the same time, the *Augustinians*, drew their inspiration from St Augustine of Hippo. In a letter of instruction to some nuns, he advised them to share everything, to pray together, and to dress without ostentation. The Augustinians tried to do the same. However, they were more flexible in their attitude than the other reformed orders, and paid more attention to the social services; schools and hospitals; the care of the poor and sick, the very young and the very old, and they also provided proper burial grounds.

The Augustine order also had its reformed versions. St Norbert (who swallowed a poisonous spider in the chalice rather than spill the consecrated wine) founded the *Premonstratensians*. Norbert was born at Cologne in 1080 and lived at court until he was thirty-five. He held various clerical posts, but regarded them only as a source of revenue until one day while out riding he was struck by lightning, and had second thoughts about his life-style.

Norbert's sudden enthusiasm for reform made him unpopular with the other clergy, so he gave all his wealth to the poor and, with the Pope's permission, travelled and preached all over Northern France. At Valenciennes he met Hugh of Fosses and in 1120, with Hugh's help, founded a community in the valley of Prémontré. St Norbert went on preaching in France and Germany, and in 1126 was made archbishop of Magdeburg where, after a rather stormy eight years, he died.

His friend Hugh succeeded him as head of the order of Premonstratensian canons. They and the Augustinian canons of which they were a branch, formed a link between the monks who lived a life of seclusion, and the itinerant preaching friars.

Another Augustinian inspired order is the one founded by St Bridget of Sweden, a strong-minded mother of eight, who had no qualms about reproving the king and queen of Sweden for their way of life, nor about offering uncompromising advice to the pope, while visiting Rome. She was guided throughout her life by visions which she carefully recorded. In 1344 she founded the Order of the Holy Saviour, later called the *Bridgettines*.

While the Augustinians had recognised the need for more contact with people outside monasteries, the idea was further developed by two men, St Dominic and St Francis of Assisi, who are often linked together but whose approach was very different. For St Dominic teaching was paramount; he was determined to reach men's minds and compel them to accept the truth. St Francis' approach was more humanitarian and he felt that too much emphasis on learning could be a barrier.

St Dominic, founder of the order of *Preaching Friars*, was born in 1170 of a noble family at Calaruega in Castile. He joined the Augustinian canons at Osma, and in 1206 was chosen to accompany the bishop on a preaching mission to the south of France where the Albigensian heresy was rife. The clergy on the spot were not having much success in their struggle with the heretics, but St Dominic threw himself wholeheartedly into the mission. It was now that he began to recognise his own gift for preaching and his ability to organise others.

After several turbulent years amid civil war, he established his headquarters at Toulouse, and began training a band of itinerant preachers. The order was recognised by the pope in 1216, and St Dominic travelled around setting up friaries. He also established an order of nuns in Rome, and sent preaching friars as far afield as Oxford. He died in his friary at Bologna in 1221. In art St Dominic is often accompanied by a dog with a torch in its mouth. The torch symbolises the light of knowledge which his preaching brought to the ignorant, and the dog is a play on words — Dominicans were nicknamed '*Domini canes,*' dogs of God. St Dominic had a deeply compassionate nature, but his rather stern intellectual manner made him a less popular saint than St Francis, who loved everybody and rejoiced in all things. It is easy to sentimentalise over St Francis because of his appealing nature.

Francis was born at Assisi in 1181, son of a wealthy cloth merchant. As a youth he was lively, cheerful and friendly, and went off lightheartedly to take part in the war between Assisi and Perugia. A spell in

St Francis of Assisi

103

prison and recurring illness made him think seriously about God. On his return to Assisi he went to the dilapidated little church of San Damiano, and as he prayed before the image of Christ, he heard a voice saying, "Francis, repair my falling house". He took the command literally and rushed home, collected some bales of cloth from his father's warehouse, sold them in the market place and returned to the church with the money. To his disappointment the priest refused the money, saying that he had made no sacrifice to obtain it and it was therefore little better than stealing.

This set-back really made him think. To his family's dismay he went to live among the beggars and lepers, caring for them as best he could. He then returned to the church at San Damiano and rebuilt it with his own hands. Francis always wore a hair shirt, walked barefoot, fasted regularly and drove himself so hard that he was often ill, but he remained cheerful always because he found beauty and love in everything. While his former companions were swearing eternal devotion to the ladies of their dreams, Francis cheerfully declared that he would serve only 'My Lady Poverty'.

A popular story tells how the people of Gubbio, terrorised by a marauding wolf, appealed to St Francis for help. While they cowered by the town gates he went out alone to find the animal. He called it, addressing it as 'Brother' wolf, and it not only came but also followed him meekly back to the town. He persuaded the inhabitants that the wolf had only killed because it was hungry, and that if they would feed it regularly it would do no more harm.

In 1210 the pope authorised Francis and eleven companions to form the order of *Friars Minor*. They renounced all possessions, even communal ones, and travelled around begging for their needs as they preached. St Francis travelled as far as the Holy Land, but his dream of converting the Saracens was not realised. The most dramatic experience of his life was the appearance on his body of scars corresponding to Christ's wounds. In art he is often shown with these 'stigmata', but more frequently he is portrayed in his more popular image of the nature-loving saint preaching to the birds.

St Clare, also born in Assisi, was twelve years younger than St Francis and a great admirer of his way of life. When her parents urged her

St Dominic

to marry, she ran away and begged St Francis to help her become a nun. He took her first to the Benedictine convent, and then helped her to found her own order at San Damiano, the *Poor Clares*, for whom he formulated a rule.

Even these hardworking, idealistic orders eventually needed reform. In 1406 Nicolette Boyer, a carpenter's daughter, had a dream in which St Francis asked her to restore the original strict rule of the Poor Clares. Although seemingly not fitted for the task, she accomplished it by determination, and her reformed order of Poor Clares is known as *Colettines*.

About the same time, St Bernardine of Siena was forming the *Observants*. After working in a hospital he became a preaching friar, and his sermons were so popular that he became known as 'the people's preacher'. Realising how disastrous it was when the poor got into the clutches of money-lenders, he organised a society to make interest-free loans. The aim of the Observants was to return to stricter observance of the Franciscan rule.

St Francis of Paola (1436-1507) went one step further. The followers of St Francis of Assisi were called Friars Minor, Little Brothers, so Francis of Paola called his order *Friars Minim*, Least Brothers. They were well known for their austerity and St Francis had a reputation for holiness which reached the ears of the king of France, Louis XI, who was seriously ill and panic-stricken at the thought of what might happen after death. Francis responded to his plea for help, went to France and settled there for the rest of his life. Sympathetic and perceptive, with a gift for mind-reading, he was nicknamed Le Bon Homme.

Matteo de Bascio (1495-1552) was an Observant who felt the need for even greater austerity. Among the changes which he made was the design of the brown habit, adding a long pointed hood. Because of this his followers were known as *Capuchins*. They are mainly a missionary order, and very strict.

Some three hundred years after the establishment of Dominicans and Franciscans, the *Society of Jesus* was formed. The founder, St Ignatius of Loyola, was born in a Basque castle in 1491, when Columbus was planning his epic voyage. Like St Francis of Assisi, he spent a carefree youth, until forced into a long convalescence by a war-wound. His leg had been fractured by a cannonball and he wiled away his time reading from a limited supply of reading matter which consisted mainly of stories about the life of Christ and the saints. He was so impressed that he resolved to give up his army ambitions and become a follower of Christ. As a token of this, when he was fit to travel he went on a pilgrimage to Montserrat and, after a night of prayer, left his sword and dagger before a statue of the Virgin. Then for a year he lived in a cave at Manresa, begging for his meagre food and never cutting his hair or nails. As he was very short (under five feet two inches) and had thick red hair, he must have been a rather alarming sight.

It was at Manresa that he mapped out his future life. First he went on pilgrimage to Jerusalem; then he spent ten years in intensive study, beginning with the Latin lessons he had neglected as a schoolboy and eventually graduating as a master of arts at Paris University.

Among Ignatius' fellow-students were seven men, including Francis Xavier, who were to form the nucleus of the Society of Jesus. In a church at Montmartre they solemnly dedicated their lives to the service of God. Their original intention was to convert the Moslems in the Holy Land, but as war between Venice and Turkey made this impossible they went to Rome instead and offered their services to the pope. With their devotion and expertise they proved extremely useful as missionaries and reformers, particularly in the field of education.

St Ignatius then produced a book, containing a rigorous course of spiritual exercises for would-be Jesuits (a name first applied disparagingly but later generally accepted) and for others who wanted guidance. The three main stages were purification (putting aside all worldly thoughts), seeking to learn God's will, and unconditional dedication. The book made a tremendous impact at the time, becoming a standard text book for study in retreats, and has been of world-wide importance ever since.

St Ignatius was the first General of the Society from 1540, when it was recognised by the pope, until his death in 1556. His main task was to direct and co-ordinate the efforts of others. In the missionary field the most outstanding work was done by one of his companions of student days, St Francis Xavier.

Like St Ignatius, St Francis was a Basque. While a student in Paris he came under the influence of St Ignatius, somewhat reluctantly, for he rather fancied himself as a future brilliant professor. St Ignatius said he was the 'lumpiest dough he had ever kneaded'! Francis Xavier was one of the original seven, and following a visit to Rome and three years work among the poor and sick, he was sent to the Far East at the request of the king of Portugal.

The voyage to India took thirteen weary months. He set up his head-quarters in Goa and spent seven years working in South India, Ceylon, Malaya and the Moluccas. In 1549 he sailed for Japan. After studying the language for a year, he was allowed to set up a mission and teach. At the end of two years he returned briefly to Goa and then sailed for China, but died on an island at the mouth of the Canton river before reaching the mainland. He was forty-six years old, and in those days of difficult travel had covered a tremendous amount of ground. Francis Xavier is credited with many miracles and making great numbers of converts, including 400,000 Japanese.

Another important religious order is that of the *Carmelites*. They claim to go back further than any of the others, as far as the Old Testament prophet Elijah. In the early Middle Ages, groups of crusaders and pilgrims settled on Mount Carmel where Elijah, the original hermit, sought refuge from King Ahab and was fed by ravens. They claimed him as their founder and a rule was drawn up by St Albert in about 1210. When wars in the Middle East forced them westwards, the Whitefriars, as they became known, settled on the Mediterranean islands of Cyprus and Sicily, in France and England, at Alnwick in Northumberland and at Aylesford in Kent.

The strict contemplative life they led produced a number of famous mystics, including St Teresa of Avila and her namesake of Lisieux. Nowadays the Carmelites have both secluded monasteries and convents, which are austere and silent, devoted entirely to prayer, also groups which are active in charity work, particularly the Carmelite Sisters dedicated to nursing and teaching.

St Teresa of Avila (1515-1582) decided as a small girl that she was destined for sainthood. Inspired by stories of the saints, she persuaded her younger brother to run away with her, intending to do battle with the Moslems and qualify for a martyr's crown. They were found and brought back, and for a time she forgot her determination. At twenty she became a nun in the Carmelite convent at Avila. Things had changed considerably since the days of Elijah and his ravens and, although St Teresa herself spent much time in contemplation and had some wonderful mystical experiences, the convent as a whole was a worldly place.

It was many years before she branched out on her own and founded a convent of strict observance, St Joseph's at Avila. In spite of ill health, she travelled all over Spain, founding more convents of the 'Discalced' (barefoot) Carmelites. She was energetic, sensible, cheerful and witty (she said that she had no time for 'sullen saints') and wrote interesting accounts of both sides of her life, the contemplative and the practical.

St Teresa (Therese) of Lisieux, (1873-1897) was a less complex character; in fact the most remarkable thing about her was her extreme simplicity. She tried to bring perfection to small, everyday tasks, and her book, 'Histoire d'une Ame,' encouraged those who could not aspire to achieving sainthood in a dramatic way.

St John of the Cross, (1542-1591), the weaver's son who was to achieve fame as a theologian and poet, was a Carmelite friar who felt the need for reform. After meeting St Teresa of Avila he threw himself enthusiastically into the formation of the Discalced order. His great suffering in prison caused him to write moving spiritual poetry. Shortly before his death the Calced and Discalced orders were separated and, very late in the day, he was recognised as co-founder with St Teresa of Avila.

In addition to the principal orders and their reformed branches, there are many smaller ones which were usually founded for charitable purposes. St Angela of Brescia, born near Lake Garda in 1474, was an orphan and had great sympathy for deprived children. As a Franciscan tertiary she realised her gift for teaching and, after pilgrimages to Rome and the Holy Land, she formed a group of nuns dedicated principally to teaching — the Company of St Ursula, Ursulines.

A contemporary of St Angela, St John of God, born in Portugal in 1495, gave up his soldier's life at the age of forty and devoted himself to the sick. After his death an order of hospitallers was formed, the *Brothers of St John of God*.

St Philip Neri, (1515-1595), although born in Florence, made his mark in Rome where he formed a brotherhood of young laymen to help pilgrims and the sick and needy. In 1551 he was ordained priest and had an oratory built over his church. Here the first 'oratorios' were sung; here too was formed the *Congregation of the Oratory*, forerunner of church clubs. St Philip encouraged the young to dance and sing, and valued kindness and cheerfulness above austerity. Genial, compassionate and hardworking, he was often criticised for his unorthodox methods, but he had a much-needed good influence on the Rome of his time.

About fifty years after the Congregation of the Oratory was set up in Rome, St Vincent de Paul did something similar in Paris. A farmer's son from the Landes, he began his career as a priest in a leisurely, luxury-loving way, but was captured by pirates and kept as a slave in Tunis for two years. After seeing the terrible condition of convicts, galley-slaves, waifs and strays and the destitute sick, he devoted himself entirely to the relief of suffering. To this end he organised groups of lay people, and also founded a society of priests called the *Congregation of the Mission*. In 1633 with the help of St Louise de Marillac, he founded at St Lazare, the *Sisters of Charity*, and in 1648, a hospital for foundlings. St Vincent de Paul is the patron saint of charitable institutions.

St Francis de Sales, (1567-1622), born in the family château near Annecy, educated at Paris and Padua, bishop of Geneva, was such an excellent writer that he became the patron saint of journalists. As well as being scholarly he was compassionate and sensitive. With St Jeanne de Chantal he founded the *Order of the Visitation*, intended mainly for women who wished to become nuns but did not want to join the more austere orders.

St John Bosco, (1815-1888), a brilliant teacher, was a great admirer of St Francis de Sales. His father died when he was a child, and coming from a poor family, he understood the difficulties of the deprived. After being ordained priest at the age of twenty-six, John Bosco devoted himself to teaching, beginning in a small way with evening

110

classes for apprentices in a Turin suburb. He was a most successful exponent of the idea that good teaching depends more on arousing interest than meting out punishment. He gathered together a group of helpers whom he called *Salesians*, after St Francis. The movement spread all over Italy and eventually became known worldwide. Girls were catered for by the Congregation of the *Daughters of Mary* which St John founded in conjunction with a Genoese peasant woman, St Mary Mazzarello.

There are so many different orders that is is difficult to tell them apart. When studying pictures it can be helpful to recognise the habits of the various orders; for instance, St Catherine of Siena wears the white habit, black mantle and white veil of a Dominican Tertiary. Benedictines wear a black habit, Carthusians white, Cistercians white with a black scapular. The Franciscan habit is brown or grey, the Dominican more distinctive — a white habit under a long black cloak and hood. Jesuits wear a straight black cassock and square cap.

CHAPTER 9

Patron Saints

In the early days of Christianity everything was clear-cut, either black or white with no comfortable greys. Anyone who truly believed felt obliged to live and die in such a way as to earn everlasting glory. The only alternative was eternal damnation.

As time went by issues became more confused. Most of the medieval saints (with a few notable exceptions) belonged to noble families, were educated at the local monastery, went on to study law and theology at Rome, Paris, Oxford or Bologna, and were familiar with the writings of earlier scholars. However, for the great mass of people who could neither read nor write, religion must have been frightening rather than inspiring. The Bible was a closed book and much of the preaching must have been above their heads. Paintings and sculptures in church, however, were something they could understand. The glorious medieval stained glass windows were not only beautiful, they made the Bible stories come alive. Pictures and statues of saints represented real human beings who had suffered on earth and would understand those still struggling here. Already safe in heaven they had access to God and would be willing to intercede. To ask help of a sympathetic saint required far less courage than a direct appeal to the Almighty.

It seemed therefore logical to address a saint who had personal experience of one's own particular problem. Blind people would feel a special affinity with St Hervé of Brittany, the wandering minstrel-monk who was blind from birth; or St Omer, blind for many years; or St Ottilia (Odilia), born blind and left to die by an impatient father but miraculously healed after baptism; or two martyrs blinded before exe-

St Roch, dressed as a Compostella Pilgrim, with his dog; Patron Saint of those with skin disorders

cution, St Leger, bishop of Autun, whose eyes were gouged out with a gimlet, or St Lucy, the fourth century virgin martyr of Syracuse.

There is a sympathetic saintly ear for every ailment from haemorrhoids (St Fiacre) to headaches (St Denis, France's national saint, who had his head chopped off — a drastic cure!) The saint for toothache, recognisable by her symbol of forceps gripping a tooth, is St Apollonia who, when very old, was brutally beaten for refusing to deny her faith, and had all her teeth knocked out. Threatened with burning, she murmured a prayer and walked voluntarily into the flames. St Hubert is invoked for protection against rabies, and St Roch (San Rocco) who worked among victims of the plague and then contracted it himself, is the saint to ask for help against skin infections and all contagious diseases.

The legend, if such it is, of St Dympna, who is invoked against insanity, and St Gerebernus, began with the discovery in the 13th century at Gheel, near Antwerp, of two sets of bones, presumably martyrs', male and female. It was said that Dympna was the daughter of a pagan Irish prince and a Christian mother. The father was distraught when his beloved wife died and developed an incestuous passion for Dympna who was growing up to look very like her mother. A priest, Gerebernus, helped her to escape to Belgium, but her father followed and, when she refused to return with him, killed them both. After the discovery of the relics it was found that people with mental illness were helped by praying at the tomb. So many sufferers flocked to the district that a hospital was built and Gheel became a centre for the treatment of nervous disorders.

St Vitus is also invoked against various nervous ailments, but his speciality is St Vitus' dance, (chorea). It is said that when as a boy he was imprisoned for his faith, he was entertained by dancing angels. A more down-to-earth explanation of the name is that crowds of mentally disturbed pilgrims at his shrine twitched and danced in mass hysteria.

St Blaise, 4th century bishop of Sebaste in Armenia, is the patron of wild animals and woolworkers as well as of throat sufferers. (The patron saint of all animals, both wild and tame, is of course St Francis of Assisi). A refugee from persecution, St Blaise took to the hills and

114

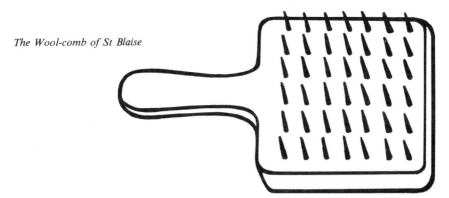

The Wool-comb of St Blaise

lived a hermit's life in a cave. He soon made friends with the wild creatures of the area and they came to him daily for blessing. Some hunters stumbling on this scene thought he must be a sorcerer and dragged him before the Roman prefect. On the way he cured a small boy choking on a fish bone, and also commanded a wolf to return a woman's pet pig that it had stolen. When the woman heard later that St Blaise had been cast into a dark dungeon, she killed her pig to provide him with meat and a candle. He was put to death in a horrible way, his flesh being scraped off his bones with the metal combs used by woolcombers. On his feast day, 3rd February, a service for throat sufferers is held in several churches, notably St Etheldreda's, Holborn, London. Two lighted candles, tied together with ribbons to form a cross, are held under the chins of those invoking his aid.

Another martyr who suffered an unusual and decidedly gruesome death was St Erasmus, also called St Elmo, whose entrails were wound out on a windlass. This naturally makes him the patron saint of stomach sufferers, and also indirectly of sailors, as his emblem, a windlass, resembles a capstan. The blue light sometimes seen on ships' masts, caused by an electrical disturbance, was called St Elmo's fire and taken as a sign of his protection.

Sailors have several other patron saints, including St Nicholas. On his feast day, 6th December, his statue is taken out in a boat at Bari, on Italy's east coast, to bless the waters. Many churches near the sea are dedicated to him, and in the days before lighthouses a burning light was positioned on a tower to guide approaching ships. Sailors in the eastern Mediterranean still say, 'May St Nicholas hold the tiller,' and those saved from shipwreck make votive offerings to him.

St Nicholas, born early in the 4th century, was supposed to be devout from birth; it is said that he refused to suck his milk on Wednesdays and Fridays, official fast days! He was one of the few early saints to escape martyrdom. As bishop of Myra in Asia Minor he lived to a ripe old age and was buried in his church there, but in 1087 Italian sailors stole his relics and took them home to Bari. He combines several duties, especially that of patron saint of children. Of the many legends about him the strangest concerns three boys chopped up and pickled by a wicked innkeeper. The saint said a prayer over the pickle-tub and the boys were made whole and restored to life. This story is believed to have arisen because of a misunderstanding; it was difficult to get any sense of perspective in early stained glass windows and the supposed boys in a tub were probably candidates for baptism.

A popular story tells how the saint rescued three sisters, who with no money for a dowry, were on the point of being sold as prostitutes when St Nicholas heard of their plight. Secretly he threw three bags of gold through their window; some say he climbed on the roof and dropped the money down the chimney, which fits in well with his more recent image as Santa Claus. The three bags of gold were adopted as their trade-sign by the bankers of Lombardy, and developed into the three gold balls of pawnbrokers.

In some places it is still the purple-robed bishop St Nicholas, riding a white horse and accompanied by his servant, Black Peter, who goes round on 5th December, the eve of his festival, putting sweets and small gifts in the shoes left out by hopeful children; sometimes they leave wisps of hay for his horse too. Dutch emigrants took the custom to the United States where he was called Santa Claus. Later he was merged with the old Father Christmas of mumming plays and became the red-robed, bewhiskered, much-commercialised figure of the present day, changing his visiting date to Christmas Eve.

When children grow too old for the special appeal of St Nicholas, they come under the protection of St Agnes and St Pancras, both martyred in their early teens. Girls who seemed in danger of reaching their twenty-fifth birthday without finding a husband, used to ask the aid of St Catherine, the scholarly virgin martyr of Alexandria, and on 25th November, her feast day, crown her statue with flowers.

St Catherine of Alexandria with her Wheel

St Fiacre

The saint for betrothed couples is St Dorothy who sent roses and apples from the gardens of Paradise to her doubting admirer. St Joseph, because of the 'no room at the inn' episode, is the patron saint of house hunters, and St Martha, the practical sister of Mary and Lazarus, of housewives. Women with troublesome husbands can have recourse to St Wilgefortis, called St Uncumber in England. This legendary Portuguese princess, determined to maintain her virginity, prayed to become less beautiful. The beard which grew on her face in answer to her prayer deterred even her most ardent suitor, the king of Sicily. Her father, furious at losing the prospect of such a good family connection, had her crucified.

There are saints to cover every manner of misfortune. St Giles, the 8th-century hermit, accidentally injured while protecting his pet hind from huntsmen, is the patron saint of cripples and beggars; St Mary Magdalene of fallen women and penitents; St Leonard of prisoners; and St Anthony of Padua of people who have lost something. On the happier side, St Christopher is the patron saint of travellers, and St Bernard of Menthon (or Montjoux) of mountaineers. As archdeacon of Aosta, St Bernard was worried about mountain travellers who had to cope with robbers as well as the usual perils of high snow-bound passes. He banished the brigands and built two hospices, staffed by Augustinian canons. The Great and Little St Bernard Passes were named after him, and so were the dogs who were later used to rescue benighted travellers.

The patron saint of musicians is St Cecilia (her feast day, 22nd November, is marked by concerts); of actors, Genesius of Rome; of artists, St Luke; of writers, St John the Evangelist, or, since 1923, St Francis de Sales. Because of his literary output during his exile on Patmos, St John is also the patron of printers, publishers and booksellers.

St Fiacre, with his emblem of a spade, is the patron of gardeners because he grew such remarkable vegetables near the hermitage and hospice that he established at Meaux in France. He would never allow women on to his land, and even after his death female trespassers were supposed to meet with misfortune. The terminus for the first hired cabs in Paris early in the 17th century was at the Hotel St-Fiacre, and the name fiacre was soon applied to the cabs that used it.

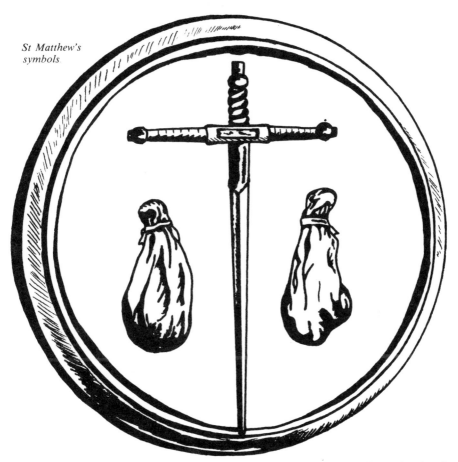

St Matthew's
symbols

Huntsmen have a choice of two saints, Eustace or Hubert, both of whom were converted by seeing a stag with a crucifix between its antlers. Anglers presumably share with fishermen the two Bethsaida brothers, Andrew and Peter, who left their nets to become 'fishers of men'. Even television viewers have a patron, St Clare of Assisi who, as she lay dying, saw as if on a television screen the Christmas Mass being celebrated in St Francis' church miles away.

Every medieval guild had its special saint, and now there seems to be one for every trade and profession. Soldiers can choose between the soldier saints George and Theodore, or St Michael the archangel. As well as a sword, St Michael carried scales for weighing the souls of the dead, and this makes him the protector of grocers. For butchers, tanners, glove-makers and furriers there is St Bartholomew who was

119

flayed alived and whose emblem is a knife. Anyone connected with finance is looked after by St Matthew, an ex-tax-collector, lawyers by St Yves (Ivo), the Breton priest who used his legal training to help the poor; carpenters by St Joseph or St Thomas; metalworkers by St Dunstan, the versatile Archbishop of Canterbury; postmen and telephone workers by Gabriel, archangel of the Annunication; domestic workers by St Zita, a model of piety and quiet efficiency; beekeepers by the two 'honeysweet doctors,' Ambrose and Bernard of Clairvaux; missionaries by St Paul or St Francis Xavier; air hostesses by St Geneviève, and shoemakers by the brothers Crispin and Crispinian, 3rd century martyrs whose feast day, 25th October, was made famous by Shakespeare's Henry V in his speech before the battle of Agincourt. Artillerymen, firework-makers, quarrymen, miners, in fact all whose work is associated with explosions, have as their patron, St Barbara, the beautiful virgin who was converted to Christianity while shut up in a tower by her jealous father. He was so angry when he heard that she had been baptised that he killed her, and was immediately struck dead himself by a thunderbolt.

The obvious choice for doctors is St Luke, the 'beloved physician,' but there are also the twin brothers, Cosmas and Damian, and the 4th-century martyr, Pantaleon. Cosmas and Damian, who lived in Syria at the end of the 3rd century, never made any charge for their services. As Christians they were condemned to death, but attempts to kill them by drowning, burning and stoning all failed and they were eventually beheaded. Long afterwards a man with a diseased leg went to sleep while praying in their church. He dreamed that they had cut off his bad leg, and when he awoke it was healed. Others who followed his example found that it worked for them too. The other doctor saint, Pantaleon, 'the all-compassionate,' was court physician to the emperor Galerius. Under Diocletian's persecution he too was condemned to death, but in his case six different methods had to be tried. Finally he died while nailed to an olive tree, which at once sprouted leaves and flowers and fruit, all at the same time. A phial of his blood preserved at Ravello, regularly liquifies like that of St Januarius.

Apart from saints for ailments and occupations, there is another very numerous group — those with a local or regional interest. People

120

who live in the shadow of Mount Etna hope that St Agatha of Catania will protect them from an eruption of the volcano as she did in the 3rd century.

In predominantly Roman Catholic countries, every town has its patron saint and his or her feast day is a time of great festivity. First the statue, dressed in rich robes, often decorated with costly jewels, and garlanded with flowers, is taken in solemn procession through the streets. After a religious service, the 'feast' starts to live up to its name, and as darkness falls the singing and dancing begin, fireworks explode, and the chuch, outlined in coloured lights, forms the back-cloth to a scene of noisy gaiety.

The saints are very much part of the life of villages and small towns, but big towns also have their patrons, although they may not be quite so conscious of them. The patron of Glasgow is St Kentigern, the 6th-century bishop who founded a church there. Legend says that as a new-born baby he was found with his mother on the seashore at Culros and taken to a monk called St Servanus who ran a school for local boys. Servanus baptised the baby and later adopted and educated him, becoming so fond of him that he called him by the affectionate nick-name Mungo (dearest) which is still used as an alternative name for the saint. Because Kentigern was so obviously the teacher's favourite the other boys gave him a rough time and he eventually ran away. He settled in Glasgow and, at the early age of twenty-five, was made bishop. Hardworking, ascetic and kind, he was respected, loved, and appealed to in all sorts of difficulties. Some of the miracles ascribed to him are recorded in the city's coat-of-arms, including a fish that found a missing ring — the saint's emblem.

The patron saint of Paris is Geneviève, who as a little girl was noticed by St Germanus as he passed through Nanterre on his way to Britain. A devout child, she received the veil when she was fifteen years old and devoted her life to charitable works. When Attila and his Huns were advancing towards Paris in 451, she persuaded the panic-stricken inhabitants not to abandon the city. The fact that Attila turned towards Orléans instead was attributed to her prayers. She gave even more practical assistance when Paris was besieged by Franks, organising and leading a convoy of boats up the Seine to

Troyes to fetch food for the starving inhabitants. She was often criticised by her own people, but the Frankish leaders, Childeric and Clovis, greatly respected her and in response to her pleas showed more mercy towards their prisoners than was usual at that time.

Many miracles were ascribed to Geneviève, and there is still an annual celebration of an event that happened in 1129; an epidemic suddenly ended when her relics were carried through the streets. Because of a story that the deveil came and blew out her candle one night when she was praying alone in church, she is usually pictured with a candle; sometimes the devil lurks nearby, holding a bellows.

Nations also have their patron saints, sometimes more than one. Italy has two — Catherine of Siena and Francis of Assisi. Portugal's patron saint, Anthony of Padua, also spent most of his life in Italy and his shrine at Padua is a place of pilgrimage, but he was actually born in Lisbon in 1195.

St James the Great, elder of the 'Sons of Thunder' and one of the three apostles most often in the company of Jesus, is the patron saint of Spain. He may have gone there as a missionary before his execution

St James the Great (right) with his Shell

in Jerusalem in 44 A.D., but the more likely story is that his bones were taken there by sea, buried at Padron, and removed for safety to Compostella — the Starlit Field.

In the long struggle to drive the Moors from Spain, St James appeared at least forty times as a knight in shining silver armour, helping and encouraging the Spanish soldiers. He was regarded as the great deliverer, the patron saint who rescued Spain from heathen tyranny and made it part of Christendom again.

Because of his arrival by sea, a cockleshell was adopted as his emblem, and worn by pilgrims as a sign that they had visited his shrine. Until fairly recently English children with only the haziest knowledge of the saint would make a little grotto of shells, moss and flowers and carry it around on 25th July, his feast day, collecting 'pennies for the grotto'.

St Denis, the patron saint of France, was Italian-born, being one of the missionaries sent to Gaul by the pope. From his headquarters on an island in the Seine he travelled the countryside, preaching and making many converts. After several successful years he and two friends were executed on Montmartre, the martyrs' hill. St Denis was supposed to have carried his own severed head to his place of burial, and this is how he is usually portrayed. The three bodies were thrown into the Seine, but recovered by a Christian woman and secretly buried. Years afterwards a Benedictine abbey was built for the relics which were kept in a silver sarcophagus. They were lost during the Revolution, but later found by a monk and restored to the abbey of Saint-Denys.

St Boniface, the apostle of Germany, was born in Crediton, Devon, in about 675. Winfred (or Winfrith) as he was then called, went to a monastery school near Exeter when he was seven, and then to another at Nursling, Hampshire. He taught Latin to his fellow monks and was a good preacher, but his great dream was to evangelise Frisia (Holland). His first attempt was abortive, as everyone was too busy with a war to listen to him, so the second time he made a greater effort to organise things better. He went to Rome where the pope promised to persuade the powerful Charles Martel to help. This worked and he was able to make great numbers of converts, especially after his dramatic ges-

123

ture of chopping down an oak tree sacred to Thor. Bystanders who expected him to be struck by a thunderbolt, were ready to listen to him when nothing happened.

Boniface was made archbishop and founded several monasteries, the most famous being at Fulda, 120 miles south-east of Cologne. In spite of his success, he still cherished his dream and at the age of 74 journeyed north to Frisia again. This time his campaign went splendidly, but one day when he was holding a mass baptism at Dokkum, there was a sudden pagan attack. The converts were surrounded and killed, St Boniface being beaten to death.

England's connection with St George is tenuous. He is believed to have been a Roman soldier, martyred at Lydda in Palestine for defying the edict of the emperor Diocletian. As a soldier saint he was popular with the crusaders who believed he helped them on more than one occasion, notably at the siege of Acre. Returning English crusaders brought the cult home with them, and in those days of endless wars, troops charged into battle with the cry, 'St George for England!' In his shining armour the saint became the personification of knightly chivalry, and inevitably was enmeshed in legend. The story of the dragon-slaying was originally set at Silene in Libya, but in time a claim was made for a hill in Berkshire, and to this day no grass grows where the dragon's blood is supposed to have been shed. St George's day, 23rd April was a public holiday from the time of Henry III. Edward III made George England's official saint and founded the Order of the Garter for forty 'men of knightly renown'. The members still attend St George's chapel, Windsor, in their striking robes on his feast day. His flag, the red cross on a white ground, is flown, and some people make the patriotic gesture of wearing a rose, but the festival is celebrated with less open excitement than those of St Andrew, St David and St Patrick. Scottish, Welsh and Irish expatriates are particularly enthusiastic about remembering their patron saints.

Scotland's St Andrew, 'first-called' of the disciples, appears less often in the Bible than his brother Peter. With little definite information about his evangelising missions, there is plenty of scope for legend. He may well have preached in Russia, whose patron saint he is, and also in Greece, but it is unlikely that he came further west. He is believed to have been martyred in Patras where his converts included the wife and brother of the Roman pro-consul who, far from following suit, had him first scourged and then tied (not nailed) to a transverse cross. It was a lingering death; the apostle survived for two whole days, during which time he continued to preach to the watching crowd and made many converts. After his death, some of them buried his body secretly. In 337 it was removed to Byzantium on Constantine's orders and in 1204 when the city was captured, the relics were taken to Amalfi. At some time between the two moves, some of the bones were supposedly stolen by a monk called Regulus who took them to Scotland. He was warmly welcomed by Nechtan, newly converted king of the Picts, and made first bishop of St Andrews. Soon afterwards while another king of the Picts, Hungus, was at war, the transverse cross of St Andrew appeared in the sky above his army, inspiring them to victory. He adopted the cross saltire as his flag, and it has remained the flag of Scotland ever since.

Ireland's patron saint may have been born in England, Wales or Scotland or possibly even Brittany, but definitely not in Ireland. The most probable location was on the bank of the Severn and the date 385. When he was about sixteen, St Patrick was captured by pirates and carried off to Ireland as a slave. For six years he was a shepherd in Antrim, a lonely life which gave him plenty of time to think about God. It also gave him another advantage over most missionaries to foreign lands — he learnt the language, so that when years later he returned to Ireland, he was able to preach in the Gaelic tongue.

While he was planning to escape, he had a dream in which he was told where to find a ship. He made his way southwards and found the promised vessel whose cargo included, strangely, a number of dogs. The captain was reluctant to take him on board until he agreed to look after the animals — no doubt his experience as a shepherd came in useful.

After landing in Gaul, where he was trained as a priest by Germanus of Auxerre, he is believed to have gone to Rome where the pope confirmed him in his desire to return as the apostle of Ireland. The previous bishop, not being able to speak the language, had made little impression. Patrick made a dramatic start in his confrontation with the pagan king Laoghaire of Tara. It was the eve of a Druid festival which required that no fires should be lit, but it was also Easter Eve. On top of Slane Hill, Patrick lit the Paschal bonfire; it blazed out defiantly in the black night.

The Druids were a force to be reckoned with, but the saint travelled all over the country, preaching, baptising and building churches. One of his helpers was St Bridget (Bride) of Kildare who was buried in the same tomb at Down Patrick. The two best-known stories about St Patrick tell how he banished snakes from Ireland and how he used the three-in-one leaves of the shamrock to explain the Trinity.

St David of Wales is one of the few home-grown patron saints. The son of Sant, a Welsh chieftain, and St Non, he spent most of his life in Wales, although he may have gone on pilgrimage to Jerusalem. He was a gifted orator; whenever he preached a white dove (his emblem) perched on his shoulder. Crowds flocked to hear him and one day the throng was so dense that those at the back could neither see nor hear. St David spread his handkerchief on the ground and immediately a hillock rose up, from the top of which he preached a sermon that could be heard by all.

He was an active campaigner against Pelagianism. In 519 at the anti-heresy Synod at Brefi, he spoke so forcefully that he was invited to become archbishop of Wales in place of St Dubricius. He was very strict, but much loved. Of the twelve monasteries that he founded in Wales, the principal one — at Menevia, now St David's — became a place of pilgrimage.

On St David's Day, 1st March, eisteddfodau (competitions in music, poetry and drama) are held, and little girls delight in wearing their national costume. The custom of wearing a leek is supposed to have arisen when Welsh soldiers snatched up the first thing that came to hand to distinguish themselves in battle from their Saxon enemies. Because 'leek' and 'daffodil' are similar in Welsh, the daffodil is considered as an alternative, and more attractive, emblem.

With all these patron saints, there should be enough to cover every eventuality. However, if all else fails, there is always St Jude — 'Judas (not Iscariot)' as he is called in the Bible. We know very little about him but he is the patron saint of lost causes, the one who brings hope to the desperate.

St Jude

127

On a number of saints' days special customs are observed, sometimes linked with an event in the saint's life, sometimes arising from confusion with a pagan festival. St Nicholas and his present-giving is an example of the former, 'Valentines' of the latter. There seem to have been two 3rd-century martyrs called Valentine, one a bishop, the other a doctor, and we know almost nothing about either. St Valentine's day, 14th February, coincided with the Roman festival of Lupercalia when partners were chosen by lot, and also with the date on which birds were traditionally supposed to choose their mates. These romantic associations gave rise to the custom of sending Valentine cards.

St Lucy, the virgin martyr of Syracuse, is associated with festivals of light, particularly in Sweden. This is partly because of her name (lux, light), partly because her feast day, 13th December, falls at the start of the month-long 'Little Yule'. Very early in the morning on Lucy Day, one girl in every home, the chosen Lucy, wearing a white dress with a red sash and a crown of lighted candles, carries coffee and saffron buns to the other members of the family. The buns are shaped like swastikas to ward off the devil and, as he can disguise himself as a cat, they are called 'Lusse cats.' Every community also has its Lucy, each with her crown of living light — very important in the cold dark Scandinavian winter.

Half-way round the year from Lucy Day is Midsummer Day, 24th June, the feast of the nativity of John the Baptist (not the anniversary of his martyrdom as is the case with most saints' days). On St John's Eve blazing bonfires are lit, supposedly to strengthen the sun which has now passed its prime.

While St Lucy and St John might be mildly surprised at the ceremonies taking place on their feast days, St Walburga would certainly be amazed at finding herself involved with witchcraft. This 8th-century abbess, born in Wessex, went to Germany at the request of St Boniface and founded an important double monastery at Heidenheim. On the night of 1st May, the anniversary of the translation of her relics to Eichstätt, witches are supposed to gather in the Hartz mountains where *Walpurgisnacht* is anything but holy. However pilgrims visit her shrine for a more saintly purpose — to see the miraculous oil which exudes from it.

128

Finally we must mention St Swithin, the gentle bishop of Winchester, tutor of King Alfred. He was so kindhearted that when he saw an old woman drop her basket of eggs he said a prayer and miraculously mended them for her. He knew that his monks would want to give him a splendid tomb when he died, so made them promise that they would bury him outside the church where the rain might fall on his grave and people walk over it. After his death they complied with his wishes, but later it was felt that he deserved something better and plans were made to rebury his bones in the cathedral. On the proposed day it began to rain so heavily that the move was postponed, and finally the idea abandoned after torrents of rain had continued to fall for forty days. This was taken as a sign that St Swithin's relics were to be left undisturbed, and gave rise to our most unreliable weather forecast:

St Swithin's day if it be fair,
For forty days 'twill rain nae mair
St Swithin's day if it does rain,
For forty days it will remain.

CHAPTER 10
The Pilgrims

Those who made the pilgrimage to Jerusalem hoped to be absolved from past sins. It seemed wise to leave it as late in life as possible, hoping that most of one's sins had already been committed and that the clean slate would have a chance of remaining unsullied. This meant that some who embarked on the journey were physically unfit, and few had any real idea of the hazards in store for them. In illustrations they look beautifully neat and tidy as they set out, but they had to face seasickness, extremes of heat and cold, hunger and thirst, desperate weariness and attacks by men and animals.

During the Roman persecution, Christians gathered at the tomb of a martyr, especially on the anniversary of his death; St Polycarp was the first saint to be regularly honoured in this manner. Then Constantine and his mother St Helena opened up the way to Jerusalem, building churches and gathering together sacred relics. Pilgrims flocked to fulfil their vows and hospices were built to accommodate them.

When Saracens overran the Holy Land, closing it to pilgrims and desecrating the sacred places, it was a great shock to Christendom. For almost four hundred years the pious and valiant dedicated their lives to driving them out, joined by the shrewd and adventurous. Returning crusaders brought back relics, often spurious, and people who could not go on pilgrimage themselves, pinned their faith on a piece of bone or a tooth or some personal possession of the saint. The ignorant and gullible were easily duped, and there was much abuse. The possession of relics brought pilgrims with offerings and made a church rich, and it was very tempting to obtain them by any means. There is a story of a

The Well of St Reine

bishop who triumphantly brought home a scrap of bone he had bitten off while kissing the relic with apparent reverence!

Priceless reliquaries were made to contain them, caskets of gold and silver, ivory and enamel, studded with gems of fabulous beauty, sometimes shaped like a head or an arm, like those of Charlemagne at Aachen, or a hand like the one at Topkapi housing the finger-bones of John the Baptist. Reliquaries are among the most costly and beautiful church treasures which have been preserved.

Next to Jerusalem in importance came Rome, seat of the pope, scene of many early matrydoms. Rich in shrines and works of art, Rome had much to offer the pilgrim. Nearer home for those living in England, France or Spain was the tomb of St James the Great, Spain's patron saint, at Santiago de Compostella.

St James of Compostella

The south coast ports of Devon and Cornwall were the favourite starting point for English pilgrims to St Jame's shrine. From all over the country they wended their way south-west, gathering at big ports like Dartmouth or Fowey, or even at small villages on the River Tamar like Bere Ferrers and Cargreen. The weary and faint-hearted settled for the island-monastery of St Michael's Mount near Penzance, but most found a ship, often one returning empty to Bordeaux after delivering a cargo of wine. From here the overland route was long but wellmarked. Others preferred the longer sea-route to Corunna which put them ashore only about two days journey on foot or horseback from their goal. There were several recognised routes; one of the gathering points was in Paris by the tour Saint-Jacques which still stands, although the pilgrim's church has disappeared. As the pilgrims reached the top of the last hill at the end of their long trek, they must have felt that their safe arrival was in itself something of a miracle. The awe-inspiring cathedral with its powerful sculpture and shining statue of St James is still worth a pilgrimage, but very much easier to reach nowadays.

The shrine of Edward the Confessor in Westminster Abbey was a popular one in the Middle Ages, and there were many others ranging from Lindisfarne in the north, to Ely in the east, and St David's in the west. The Pilgrims' Ways can still be followed, and there are reminders of those devout travellers in wayside crosses. springs where they refreshed themselves and inns called *Pilgrims' Rest*.

For the less ambitious there were holy wells. Cornwall, with its many saints, has a great selection of these. The one at Altarnun where St David's mother, St Non, is supposed to have died, was believed to cure the insane; miracles apart, sudden immersion in the ice-cold water was no doubt equivalent to modern shock-therapy!

In the Cotswolds, two springs were associated with St Kenelm, the seven-year-old prince of Mercia murdered by order of his older sister. He was a pious child and died singing the *Te Deum*. The murder might have remained undiscovered, had not a dove flown to Rome carrying in its beak a scroll describing what had happened. It dropped the scroll at the pope's feet and an investigation was ordered. The boy's body was found on a lonely hillside. One spring gushed up where it had lain, and another appeared where the bearers rested as they were carrying it to Winchcombe for burial.

The well at Holywell, Flint, is attributed to St Winifred, only child of a Welsh chieftain. While resisting rape she had her head struck off, but her uncle, himself a saint, put it back on and restored her to life. Only a thin white line on her neck showed where it had been severed.

The most popular of all English shrines is that of St Thomas à Becket at Canterbury, and Chaucer immortalised many of the pilgrims in his *Canterbury Tales*.

When Henry II came to the English throne in 1154, the country needed a strong ruler. The last thing Henry wanted was interference

Wayside Cross on a Pilgrim Route

from the pope. In order to retain control of church affairs it seemed a good idea to appoint his friend, Thomas à Becket, Archbishop of Canterbury. Although Thomas accepted the position reluctantly and warned that he would have to obey the dictates of conscience rather than friendship, Henry was dismayed and furiously angry when Thomas opposed him. "Will no one rid me of this turbulent priest?" he shouted.

Henry probably had no intention of being taken literally, but four of his knights immediately rode off to Canterbury and murdered St Thomas in his cathedral, on the 29th December 1170, a memorable date for Canterbury. Everyone was shocked, including the king. It was a great blow to his popularity and when the war in Scotland started to go badly, it seemed that everything was against him. He decided to do public penance, walking barefoot through the streets of Canterbury and kneeling all night by the martyr's tomb while monks beat him with rods.

Soon it was claimed that miracles were being wrought at the shrine. St Thomas' fame spread far and wide and pilgrims came with their pleas and their offerings. Louis VII, king of France, came to pray for the recovery of the fifteen-year old Dauphin who was seriously ill. His prayer was answered and in gratitude he gave a magnificent gold goblet and promised a yearly gift of wine.

Other treasures flowed in, making the church extremely rich. The relics were placed in a priceless gold casket, elaborately wrought and studded with jewels. Unfortunately like so many other treasures, it was destroyed at the time of the Reformation.

One of the best-loved saints is St Anthony of Padua, patron of the poor and downtrodden and also, because he was an ardent seeker after lost souls, of losers, whether the loss be a thimble or a fortune. Born at Lisbon in 1195, he became an Augustinian canon at fifteen. Ten years later, with dreams of becoming a missionary and perhaps a martyr, he joined the Franciscan friars. His first mission was to Morocco, but ill-health forced him to return home. Contrary winds drove the ship to Italy where he met St Francis of Assisi, fourteen years his senior. He remained in Italy, preaching to such good effect that he was called 'the hammer of the heretics'. It was sometimes uphill work; it is said that when the people of Rimini refused to listen to him, he preached instead to the fish who came in shoals to hear him.

St Anthony led a life of outstanding purity, symbolised in art by a lily, and had frequent visions of the Christ-child with whom he is usually portrayed. In art the beauty and gentleness of his features is emphasised, and it is easy to overlook his inner strength and resilience.

St Anthony died at the age of thirty-six and was buried at Padua. When his relics were moved more than thirty years later, it was found that his tongue, unlike the rest of his flesh, had remained free from decay. This made a tremendous impression and countless pilgrims have sought, and been granted, a miracle at his shrine.

Other miraculous happenings which still draw pilgrims are the excuding of oil from the shrine of St Walburga (Walpurgis) at Eichstätt and the liquifying of St Pantaleon's blood at Ravello. The blood of San Gennaro (St Januarius), patron saint of Naples, also liquifies and interested Neapolitans wait anxiously to see how long it takes, believing that the quicker the process the better will be the year that follows.

More often people go to seek a personal miracle. The shrine of St Teresa of Lisieux is a popular one; so is that of Germaine, Cousin of Pibrac, whose body was found to be well preserved when exhumed after forty-three years. Some shrines are visited by people with a particular type of disability; Odilienberg by the blind, for example, and St Dympna's tomb at Gheel by those suffering from nervous disorders.

Undoubtedly the contemporary pilgrimage most favoured by those who need healing, physical or spiritual, is the annual one to Lourdes. The feast day of St Bernadette of Lourdes is the 16th April. Bernadette Soubirous was a miller's daughter, working as a domestic servant. In 1858 she came home to prepare for confirmation, and one day while wandering alone near the River Gave, saw a beautiful young lady standing in a cave. The lady told her, "I am the Immaculate Conception", and pointed out a spring of clear water which Bernadette had not noticed before.

At first no one would believe the story; why should the Virgin appear to a simple village girl? Over a period of six months Bernadette saw the vision eighteen times, and was so positive and unshakeable in the face of hostile questioning that at last her story was accepted, especially when miraculous healings began to occur at the grotto. St Bernadette became a nun at Nevers where she led a saintly life, enduring both criticism and ill-health with patience and dignity. A basilica was built over the grotto before she died in 1879, but she took no part in the ensuing publicity.

One of the most unusual shrines is the Santa Casa at Loreto near Ancona in Italy. It seems that the house at Nazareth in which the angel Gabriel appeared to the Virgin was in danger of being destroyed by the Turks in the late 13th century. Angels moved it bodily, first to a hill in Dalmatia, then to an Italian laurel grove (hence the name Loreto) and finally to its present spot. It became a great pilgrimage centre and the town of Loreto grew up round it. It contains a small black wooden carving of the Virgin and child, believed by some to be the work of St Luke.

Equally remarkable is the shrine at Little Walsingham in Norfolk. In 1061 Lady Richeldis de Faverches, widowed lady of the manor, was told in a dream to make a replica of the house of the Virgin. She was

St Mark's Winged Lion adorning a pillar

137

given precise measurements and had the house built exactly according to instructions. The angels apparently disapproved of the first site and moved the building during the night. It drew thousands of pilgrims. Many would stop at the Slipper Chapel at Houghton St Giles and take off their shoes to walk the last mile barefoot. A priory of Augustinian canons was founded there, but both priory and shrine were destoyed at the Reformation. In 1931 a new shrine was begun and now draws crowds of visitors.

The gold and jewels of medieval church treasure were a far cry from the simple altars of the earliest days, inscribed at most with a name and date, and perhaps one of the Christian symbols — a fish, a lamb, an anchor or the Chi-Ro symbol. There was no room for ostentation when the very fact of being a Christian was punishable by death.

Gradually churches became bigger and more richly decorated. The simple stone altars developed into elaborately painted and gilded pieces of exquisite craftsmanship. Wealthy people tried to buy salvation by giving money to the church and relics attracted pilgrims, penitents and pleaders, with their offerings, so that the medieval cathedrals, with their paintings, sculptures and stained glass windows became treasurehouses of beauty. It then became fashionable for the rich to patronise artists, and since they found most of their inspiration in religion, pictures of saints proliferated.

St Gregory remarked that there was a danger that holy pictures and statues might become idols, but that if this danger could be avoided, they would be as useful to the illiterate as books were to the scholar. St Augustine used a holy picture as a starting point when he landed in Kent on his evangelising mission.

The history of art up to quite recent times is a history of Christian art. The main feature of Byzantine art is its glorious mosaics, glowing pictures made of tiny squares of glass and marble, with soft greens, reds and blues on a sparkling gold background. The originals date from the 5th century, early enough for people to remember what the saints actually looked like. To this period also, belong the first icons, portraits on wood which, since they are supposed to be true likenesses, are valuable guides as to the actual appearance of the saints.

As permanent as the Byzantine mosaics, are the Florentine frescoes.

These too have to be visited *in situ*, but fortunately as the saints have inspired artists (and sculptors) from Giotto onwards, there are thousands of great paintings and statues in museums, art galleries and churches which can be seen today. Go into any little village church and you will find many of them there — St Peter with his keys, St John the Baptist with his lamb and scroll, St Paul with his sword and book, St Catherine with her wheel, St Jerome with his lion, the evangelists with their winged symbols, the martyrs with their palms, the pure in heart with their lilies, the founders with their model churches. They are a glorious company and worth getting to know.

Biographical Notes

Adrian (and Natalia): Martyrs. Feast Day, 8 September. Died 304. Adrian: Roman Soldier, impressed by courage of persecuted Christians; converted; imprisoned. Wife Natalia dressed as boy to visit him in prison. Adrian's limbs hacked off on anvil, then burned. In art, soldier with anvil.

Agatha: Martyr. Feast Day, 5 February. Died 250, Catania. In art, holding pincers, or breasts on dish.

Agnes: Martyr. Feast Day 21 January. Died c. 300, Rome. Symbol, lamb.

Aidan: Missionary. Feast Day 31 August. Born Ireland. Died Bamburgh, 651. Emblem, stag.

Alban: Martyr. Feast Day 17 June. First British martyr. Died c. 209 or 303, Verulamium (now St Albans). In art, decapitated.

Alphege: Martyr. Feast Day 19 April. Archbishop of Canterbury. Died Greenwich, 1012.

Ambrose: Bishop, Doctor of Church. Feast Day 7 December. Born Trèves (Trier) c. 340. Died Milan 397. Symbol, beehive.

Anastasia: Martyr. Feast Day 25 December. Died c. 304, Sirmium (then Pannonia, now Yugoslavia). Worked for imprisoned Christians. One of several put on board ship which was scuttled but returned safely to port. Later burned.

Anastasius: Martyr. Feast Day 22 January. Died 628, Caesarea. Soldier in Persian army which captured Jerusalem. Entered monastery. Went to Caesarea to preach to army. Beaten with clubs, then strangled. Relics in Rome.

Andrew: Apostle. Feast Day 30 November. Died c. 70. Emblem, transverse cross (Saltire).

Andrew Corsini: Bishop. Feast Day 4 February. Born Florence, 1301. Died Fiesole 1373. Quarrelsome youth. Converted by sight of mother in tears before statue of Virgin, praying for him. Reluctantly made Bishop of Fiesole. Good at settling disputes.

140

Angela of Brescia: Feast Day 27 January. Born Desenzano (Lake Garda) 1474. Died Brescia 1540. Left an orphan, joined Franciscan tertiaries. Successful teacher of young children. Founded Ursuline nuns.

Ann: Feast Day 26 July. Mother of Virgin.

Anselm: Archbishop of Canterbury. Feast Day 21 April. c. 1033-1109.

Anscarius: Missionary. Feast Day 3 February. Born Amiens 801. Died Bremen 865. French monk; first missionary to Denmark and Sweden.

Anthony: Abbot. Feast Day 17 January. Born 251. Died 356. Emblems, pig and bell.

Anthony of Padua: Feast Day 13 June. Born Lisbon, 1195. Died Padua, 1231. In art, holds Christ-child, lily and book.

Apollonia: Martyr. Feast Day 9 February. Died Alexandria 249. Emblem, forceps gripping tooth.

Athanasius: Bishop, Doctor of Church. Feast Day 2 May. Born and Died Alexandria, 296-375.

Aubert of Avranches: Bishop. Feast Day 10 September. 8th century. Three times dreamed that St Michael told him to build a church on the Mont St Michel. Finally did so; it was completed in 709 and he was buried there.

Audrey: (see Etheldreda).

Augustine of Canterbury: Archbishop. Feast Day 27 May. Died Canterbury 605.

Augustine of Hippo: Bishop and Doctor. Feast Day 28 August. Born Thagaste 354. Died Hippo (Now Bone) 430.

Barbara: Martyr. Feast Day 4 December. 3rd century. Emblems, palm and tower.

Barnabas: Apostle, Evangelist. Feast Day 11 June. Called apostle although not one of the Twelve. Carries St Matthew's Gospel.

Basil: Bishop and Doctor. Feast Day 14 June. Born and died Caesarea in Cappadocia, 330-379.

Bavon: Hermit. Feast Day 1 October. Born Brabernt 589. Died 653. Ancestor of Charlemagne, rich nobleman, fierce and wild until his wife died. Converted by St Amand. Gave away possessions; entered monastery; did penance for seven years living in the trunk of a hollow tree.

Bede, Venerable: Born Northumbria 633. Died Jarrow-on-Tyne 735. Historian rather than saint.

Bee: Nun. 7th century. Name preserved only in St Bees, Cumberland.

Benedict: Father of Western monasticism. Feast Day 11 July. Born Nursia (Umbria) c. 480. Died Monte Cassino c. 547. Emblem, broken cup.

Benedict Biscop (Benet): Abbot. Feast Day 12 January. Born Northumbria 628. Died Wearmouth 690. Noble at court of King Oswy. Aged 25 went to

Rome with St. Wilfrid. Became monk at Lerins, near Cannes. Sent to Canterbury with St Theodore. Went north and founded monasteries at Wearmouth and Jarrow. Great book collector, his libraries helped St Bede.

Bernadette: Feast Day 16 April. Born Lourdes 1844. Died Nevers 1879.

Bernard of Clairvaux: Abbot, Doctor of the Church. Feast Day 20 August. Born near Dijon 1090. Died Clairvaux 1153. Emblem, beehive.

Bernard of Menthon (or Montjoux): Feast Day 28 May. 11th century. Founded hospices for travellers in Alps.

Bernardine of Siena: Priest. Feast Day 20 May. Born Siena 1380. Died Aquila 1444.

Birinus: Missionary. Feast Day 5 December. Died Dorchester 650. Monk from Rome, converted pagans of Wessex. First bishop of Dorchester.

Blaise: Martyr. Feast Day 3 February. 4th century. Lived in Sebaste, Armenia.

Bonaventure: Cardinal, Doctor of the Church. Feast Day 14 July. Born Bagnorea (Umbria) 1221. Died Lyons 1274.

Boniface of Crediton: Martyr. Feast Day 5 June. Born Crediton (Devon) 675. Died Friesland, 755. Patron saint of Germany. Symbol, axe in tree.

Botolph: Abbot. Feast Day 17 June. Died 680. With brother Adolph left England to become monk in Gaul. On return founded monastery in Lincolnshire, Boston is derived from *Botolph's stone*. Popular English medieval saint with many churches dedicated to him.

Brendan: Abbot. Feast Day 16 May. Born Kerry 486. Died 578. Sailed to Land of Promise.

Bride (Bridget, Brigid): Of Kildare: Abbess. Feast Day 1 February. Born 450. Died 525. Beautiful, cheerful, hard-working, compassionate. Baptised by St Patrick. Founded first Irish convent at Kildare. Revered next to St Patrick. In art, holds candle and cross, symbolising the way in which she spread the light of Christianity.

Bridget (Brigetta) of Sweden: Feast Day 8 October. Born Sweden 1303. Died Rome 1373. Patron saint of Sweden. Emblem, heart marked with cross.

Brieuc: Abbot. Feast Day 1 May. 6th century. One of the Welsh missionaries. Born Cardiganshire, went to Brittany (via Cornwall); founded monastery at Treguier.

Bruno: Feast Day 6 October. Born Cologne 1033. Died Calabria 1101. Founder of Carthusians.

Budoc: Missionary. Feast Day 8 December. 6th century.

Cadoc: Abbot. Feast Day 25 September. 6th century. Founded Llancarfan monastery near Cardiff.

Catherine of Alexandria: Martyr. Feast Day 25 November. 4th century. Emblems, wheel and sword.

Catherine of Siena: Mystic. Feast Day 30 April. Born Siena 1347. Died Rome 1380. In art, wears white habit and black mantle of Dominicans; holds lily and book.

Cecilia: Martyr. Feast Day 22 November. 3rd century. Patron saint of musicians. Emblem, portable organ.

Chad: Bishop. Feast Day 2 March. Born Northumbria. Died Lichfield 672. Brother of Cedd who founded Lastingham Abbey. Both trained by St Aidan at Lindisfarne. Chad became bishop of Lichfield.

Charles Borromeo: Cardinal. Feast Day 4 November. Born Arona 1538. Died Milan 1584. Monk at 12 and cardinal at 22. Cared for sick and poor, especially during plague. Keen educationist; vigorous reformer.

Christopher: Martyr. Feast Day 25 July. 3rd century. Patron saint of travellers. In art, carrying Christ-child.

Clare of Assisi: Foundress of Poor Clares. Feast Day 12 August. Born and died Assisi 1194-1253.

Clement: Pope, Martyr. Feast Day 23 November. 1st century. Emblem, anchor.

Clotilda: Queen. Feast Day 3 June. Born Lyons 474. Died Tours 545. Wife of Clovis, heathen king of Franks. Prayed for his conversion. Clovis converted when he avoided defeat in battle by calling on Clotilda's God; baptised at Rheims on Christmas Day 496. Clotilda had vision of angel bringing her three feathers which gave rise to the symbol of the Fleur-de-lys. Widowed, she retired to Tours, died aged 71.

Cloud: Abbot. Feast Day 7 September. Lived 520-560. Grandson of Clovis and Clotilda. Two years old when father killed. Wicked uncles killed his older brothers and divided kingdom. No wish to regain it. Became priest. Built monastery at Saint Cloud near Paris.

Colette: Nun. Feast Day 6 March. Born Corbie 1381. Died Ghent 1447. Carpenter's daughter. Poorly educated but devout and determined. Had vision of St Francis and became a Poor Clare; reformed many convents and founded 17 new ones of strict observance.

Columba: Missionary. Feast Day 9 June. Born Donegal 521. Died Iona 597.

Columban: Abbot, Missionary. Feast Day 23 November. Born Leinster 540. Died Bobbio 615. Irish monk sent in middle age to evangelise Vosges area. Made enemies at court; threatened with deportation; moved to Lake Constance. Crossed Alps when over 70. Founded famous abbey at Bobbio 614. Emblem, bear.

Corentin: Hermit. Feast Day 12 December. 6th century. Lived in forest. Each day cut one slice from fish which then swam away. Popular in Brittany, especially at Quimper where he was first bishop.

Cosmas and Damian: Martyrs. Feast Day 27 September. Late 3rd century, Syria. Twin brothers. Patron saints of physicians.

143

Crispin and Crispinian: Martyrs. Feast Day 25 October. Patron saints of shoemakers.

Cuby: Missionary. Feast Day 8 November. 6th century. Born Cornwall. Died Anglesey.

Cuthbert: Bishop. Feast Day 20 March. Born Northumbria 634. Died Farne 687.

Cyprian: Martyr. Feast Day 16 September. Born Tunisia 200. Died Carthage 258. Lawyer, then bishop. Martyred under Valerian.

Cyprian and Justina: Martyrs. Feast Day 26 September. 4th century, Antioch. Cyprian, a sorcerer, tried to tempt virgin Justina. Converted by her. Both tortured under Diocletian. Survived being thrown into cauldron of boiling pitch; eventually beheaded.

Cyril and Methodius: Missionaries. Feast Day 7 July. Brothers, born Salonika early 9th century; missionaries to Moravia.

Damasus: Pope. Feast Day 11 December. Born and died Rome 304-384. Fought Arianism; ordered St Jerome to translate New Testament into Latin; restored catacombs and martyrs' tombs.

Damian: (see Cosmas).

David: Bishop. Feast Day 1 March. 6th century. Patron saint of Wales.

Denis: Martyr. Feast Day 9 October. 3rd century. Patron saint of France. In art, carries own head.

Desiderius of Vienne, (Didier): Bishop. Feast Day 23 May. 7th century. Reproved by pope for teaching grammar (too profane!). Made enemies at court. Killed on way to prison.

Diego: Franciscan laybrother. Feast Day 13 November. Born and died Spain 1400-1463.

Dominic: Founder. Feast Day 4 August. Born Castile 1170. Died Bologna 1221. Symbol, dog with torch.

Dorothy: Martyr. Feast Day 6 February. 4th century. Symbol, basket of fruit and flowers.

Dubricius (Dyfrig): Bishop. Feast Day 14 November. Welsh saint who is supposed to have crowned King Arthur. First bishop of Llandaff, near Cardiff.

Dunstan: Archbishop. Feast Day 19 May. Born Glastonbury 910. Died Canterbury 988. In art, holds devil's nose in tongs.

Dympna: Martyr. Feast Day 15 May. 7th century. Born Ireland. Died near Antwerp. Patron saint of insane.

Edmund: King. Feast Day 20 November. 841-869. Christian king of East Anglia. Defeated by Danes at Hoxne in Suffolk. Tied to a tree and shot with arrows, then beheaded. Head supposedly guarded by wolf, sometimes pictured with him. Body enshrined at Bury St Edmunds; abbey built there 1020. Emblem, arrow.

Edmund of Abingdon: Archbishop of Canterbury. Feast Day 16 November. Born Abingdon 1170. Died Pontigny 1246.

Edward the Confessor: King. Feast Day 13 October. Born Islip near Oxford 1004. Died Westminster 1066. Spent most of his time in Normandy until he became king in 1042. Pious, ascetic, peace-loving; called 'Confessor' because his way of life bore witness to Christ. Once met pilgrim who asked for his ring; 20 years later it was returned to him by another pilgrim. In the Holy Land the pilgrim said he had met a man who claimed to be St John the Evangelist and who asked him to return the ring to the king and warn him to prepare for his death. Edward was buried at Westminster where his relics are still preserved. First monarch credited with ability to cure scrofula, the *King's Evil*, by touch. Emblem, ring.

Elizabeth: 1st century. Mother of John the Baptist.

Elizabeth of Hungary: Queen. Feast Day 19 November. 1207-1231. Married at 14 to Louis IV of Thuringia. Widowed in 1227, with her baby and three other children she was turned out of Wartburg castle by her brother-in-law who seized the throne. Became Franciscan Tertiary; worked herself to death caring for the poor and sick; died aged 24.

Elmo, (Erasmus): Martyr. Feast Day 2 June. Died 303.

Eloi, (Eligius): Bishop. Feast Day 1 December. Born Limoges 588. Died Noyon 660. Skilled goldsmith. Founded monasteries and convents. Made reliquaries for church. Patron saint of metal-workers.

Ethelburga of Barking: Abbess. Feast Day 12 October. Died 678. First abbess of first Benedictine convent in England.

Etheldreda, (Audrey): Abbess. Feast Day 23 June. Born 630. Died Ely 679. Twice married; refused to consummate second marriage and entered convent. Built monastery at Ely; numerous miracles ascribed to her. Fair held annually on her feast day (St Audrey's fair) at which cheap baubles were sold and thus the word 'tawdry' was coined.

Etienne: (See Stephen of Grandmont).

Eugenia: Martyr. Feast Day 25 December. 3rd century. Historical facts lost. Legend asserts that she entered a monastery dressed as a man, but had to reveal her sex to refute a charge of adultery.

Eulalia: Martyr. Feast Day 10 December. Died Merida (Spain) 304. Well-known Spanish saint, tortured and martyred at age of 12. At moment of death her soul emerged from her mouth like a dove and flew to heaven.

Eustace: Martyr. Feast Day 20 September. Martyred by Trajan. Emblem, stag with crucifix between its horns.

Faith (Foy): Martyr. Feast Day 6 October. 3rd century.

Felix of Cantalice: Feast Day 18 May. Born Cantalice 1513. Died Rome 1587. Capuchin monk, first to be canonised. When given task of begging for monastery's bread was given a loaf by the Christ-child.

Ferdinand III: King of Castile. Feast Day 30 May. 1199-1252. Ousted Saracens from Spain. Founded university of Salamenca.

Fiacre: Hermit. Feast Day 30 August. 7th century. Emblem, spade.

Foy: (See Faith).

Francis of Assisi: Feast Day 4 October. 1181-1226. Founder of Friars Minor.

Francis of Paola: Feast Day 2 October. Born Paola 1436. Died Plessis-les-Tours 1507. Founder of Friars Minim. Nicknamed *Le Bon Homme*.

Francis Borgia: Jesuit. Feast Day 10 October. Born Gandia 1510. Died Rome 1972. Spanish Nobleman. Joined Society of Jesus. Father General for last seven years of his life.

Francis de Sales: Bishop. Feast Day 29 January. Born Annecy 1567. Died Lyons 1622. Co-founder with Jeanne de Chantal of Order of Visitation of Mary. Patron saint of journalists.

Francis Xavier: Missionary. Feast Day 3 December. Born Pamplona 1506. Died 1552 on way to China.

Frideswide: Abbess. Feast Day 19 October. 8th century. Patron saint of Oxford. Founded convent at Oxford on site of Christ Church.

Gabriel: Archangel. Feast Day 29 September (shared with Michael and Raphael). Patron saint of postal workers.

Gall: Missionary monk. Feast Day 16 October. 7th century. Went from Ireland to Europe with St Columban. Settled in Switzerland and set up hermitages there.

Genesius of Rome: Actor. Feast Day 25 August. 4th century. Converted; refused to recant and was executed.

Geneviève: Patron saint of Paris. Feast Day 3 January. Born Manterre 420. Died Paris 500. Symbol, book and candle.

George: Patron saint of England. Feast Day 23 April. 4th century.

Gerard of Brogne: Abbot. Feast Day 3 October. 895-959. Built monastery on his own land near Namur; asked to reform other Benedictine monasteries; some monks found him too strict and moved from France to Bath.

Germaine: Cousin of Pibrac, shepherdess. Feast Day 15 June. 1579-1601. Had withered hand; cruelly treated by stepmother and mocked by neighbours. When accused by stepmother of stealing a loaf to give to the poor, opened her apron and it was full of flowers. (Story also told of St Elizabeth of Hungary). Found dead under the stairs. Body still preserved when exhumed 43 years later. Miracles of healing have taken place at her grave, a place of pilgrimage.

Germanus of Auxerre: Bishop. Feast Day 31 July. Born Auxerre 378. Died Ravenna 448.

Gildas: Writer. Feast Day 29 January. 6th century. Studied in Wales and settled in Brittany.

Giles (Gilles): Hermit. Feast Day 1 September. Probably 8th century. Shrine near Arles was popular place of pilgrimage. Had pet hind and was accidentally wounded while protecting it from huntsmen. Over 150 churches dedicated to him in Britain. Chalfont St Giles in Buckinghamshire named after him. Patron saint of cripples; (St Giles Cripplegate, London, built 1090). Emblem, hind.

Gotthard: Bishop. Feast Day 4 May. 960-1038 Bavaria. Founder and reformer of monasteries. Pass and hospice named after him.

Gregory the Great: Pope. Feast Day 12 March. Born and died Rome 540-604. Doctor of the Church.

Gregory of Nazianzus: Theologian. Feast Day 9 May. Born and died Cappedocia 329-389. Doctor of Eastern Church.

Gregory of Tours: Bishop. Feast Day 17 November. Born Clermond-Ferrand 538. Died Tours 594.

Harvey (Hervé): Abbot. Feast Day 17 June. 6th century. Venerated mainly in Brittany. Wandering monk, blind from birth.

Helena: Empress. Feast Day 18 August. Born 250 (birthplace thought to be Colchester). Died Nicomedia 330. Mother of Emperor Constantine. Inspired by a dream to search for and find remains of True Cross.

Helier: Martyr. Feast Day 16 July. 6th century. Born in Belgium. Lived as hermit on Jersey. Murdered by pirates.

Hilarion: Hermit. Feast Day 21 October. Born Gaza 291. Died Cyprus 371. Lived as hermit for 50 years.

Hilary of Poitiers: Bishop. Feast Day 14 January. Born and died Poitiers 315-367. Doctor of Church.

Hilda: Abbess. Feast Day 17 November. Born Northumbria 614. Died Whitby 680. Of royal blood. Founded mixed monastery at Whitby.

Hippolytus: Feast Day 13 August. Confusion over two saints; one, 3rd century theologian and martyr — other legendary gaoler of St Lawrence (converted by him, buried his body, then martyred by being tied to four horses and dragged apart).

Hubert: Bishop. Feast Day 3 November. 656-727. Wild young noble; while hunting saw stag with crucifix between horns (like St Eustace). Became hermit, then bishop.

Hugh of Lincoln: Bishop. Feast Day 17 November. Born Avalon (Burgundy) 1135. Died Lincoln's Inn, London 1200. Hard-working, fearless, gentle with children and animals. Symbol, swan.

Ia: Patron saint of St Ives, Cornwall. Sailed from Ireland to Cornwall on leaf.

Ignatius of Antioch: Martyr. Feast Day 1 February. Died Rome, early 2nd century.

Ignatius Loyola: Founder of Society of Jesus. Feast Day 31 July. Born Loyola (Spain) 1491. Died Rome 1556.

Illtyd: Abbot. Feast Day 6 November. Early 6th century. Welsh saint, established monastic school at which St Samson was a pupil.

Irenaeus: Bishop of Lyons. Feast Day 3 July. Born Smyrna 130. Died 202.

Isidore the Labourer: Feast Day 10 May. Born and died Madrid 1070-1130. His master refused to allow him time off for prayer until one day found him praying and two angels doing the ploughing. Many miracles attributed to him. Patron saint of Madrid. Emblem, sickle.

Isidore of Seville: Bishop. Feast Day 4 April. Born Cartegena 560. Died Seville 636. Educationist and influential writer.

Ita: Abbess. Feast Day 15 January. 6th century. Lived County Limerick. In charge of school at which St Brendan received his early education.

Ivo of Kermartin: (See Yves).

James the Great: Apostle. Feast Day 25 July. Martyred Jerusalem 44 AD. Symbol, cockle shell.

James the Less: Apostle. Feast Day 1 May. Martyred Jerusalem 62 AD. Symbol, club.

Januarius (Gennaro): Martyr. Feast Day 19 September. Died Pozzonoli 305. Bishop of Benevento. Thrown to the lions but they would not touch him; then beheaded. Glass phial of his blood preserved in Naples cathedral; liquefaction known to have happened regularly for over 500 years. Symbol, phials on a book.

Jeanne de Chantal: Foundress. Feast Day 21 August. Born Dijon 1572. Died Moulins 1641. Married to Baron de Chantal, widowed in 1600. Close friend of Francis de Sales; founded Order of the Visitation for women not wishing to join stricter orders.

Jerome: Doctor of the Church. Feast Day 30 September. Born Dalmatia 342. Died Bethlehem 420. In art, with lion, either as ragged hermit or wearing cardinal's hat.

Joachim: Father of the Virgin. Feast Day 16 August.

Joan of Arc: Feast Day 30 May. Born Domrémy 1412. Died Rouen 1431.

John the Baptist: Forerunner of Jesus. Feast Day 24 June. Beheaded c. 29 AD by Herod Antipas for Salome. Symbols, long cross, scroll with '*Ecce Homo*', lamb.

John the Evangelist: Apostle. Also called 'the Divine'. 1st century. Brother of James the Great. Symbol, eagle; also snake in chalice.

John Bosco: Founder of Salesians. Feast Day 31 January. Born Piedmont 1815. Died Turin 1888. Educationist.

John Chrysostom: (Golden Mouth) Doctor of the Church. Feast Day 27 January. Born Antioch 347. Died Comana in Pontus 407.

John of the Cross: Spanish theologian and poet. Feast Day 24 November. Born Avila 1542. Died Ubeda 1591.

John of God: Patron saint of hospitals, nurses, and the sick. Feast Day 8 March. Born Portugal 1495. Died Granada 1559. Founded orphanages and hospitals. Work carried on after his death and order of Brothers of St John of God was formed.

John Ogilvie: Martyr. Born Banffshire 1579. Died Glasgow 1615. Canonised 17 October 1976.

Joseph: Husband of Virgin. Feast Days 19 March and 1 May.

Joseph of Arimathaea: Feast Day 17 March. 1st century. Said to have been sent by St Philip as missionary to Britain and to have founded first church at Glastonbury where his staff became the famous Christmas-flowering thorn.

Jude (Thaddeus): Apostle. Feast Day 28 October. 1st century. Patron saint of the desperate.

Julia: Martyr. Feast Day 22 May. 5th century virgin. Slave of Carthaginian merchant who took her to Corsica. Martyred for refusing to sacrifice to heathen gods. Patron saint of Corsica.

Julian: Feast Day 12 February. Accidentally killed parents. He and his wife went to live by river and, like St Christopher, helped people across it. One day he helped Christ in the guise of an old man who told them Julian's penance was over; soon after this Julian and his wife died.

Julian of Antioch: Martyr. Feast Day 16 March. Martyred under Diocletian by being put in sack full of snakes and cast into sea. Relics taken to Antioch where St John Chrysostom preached sermon in his honour. Patron saint of Rimini.

Justin: Martyr. Feast Day 14 April. Born in Palestine of Greek family. Beheaded in Rome c. 100 for refusing to sacrifice.

Kenelm: Prince of Mercia. Murdered by order of his older sister. Spring gushed up where body lay and another appeared where the bearers rested as they were carrying the body to Winchcombe (in the Cotswolds) for burial.

Kentigern (Mungo): Bishop. Feast Day 14 January. 6th century. Patron saint of Glasgow.

Keyne: Feast Day 8 October. Associated with South Wales, Herefordshire and Cornwall where she has a holy well.

Lambert: Martyr. Feast Day 17 September. Born Maestricht 635. Died Liege 705. Became bishop of Maestricht in 670. Established churches throughout Belgium.

Lawrence: Martyr. Feast Day 10 August. Died Rome 258. Symbol, gridiron.

Lawrence of Brindisi: Theologian. Linguist, Missionary. Feast Day 21 July. Born Brindisi 1559. Died Lisbon 1619. Led troops against Turks in Hungary, carrying crucifix.

Leo the Great: Pope. Feast Day 11 April. Died Rome 461. Doctor of the Church.

Leonard: Hermit. Feast Day 6 November. 6th century. Became hermit near Limoges. Saved life of Queen by prayer; given land at Noblac (St Leonard) to build monastery. Patron saint of prisoners, many of whom he tried to help.

Louis IX of France: King. Feast Day 25 August. Born Poissy 1215. Died Tunis on crusade 1270.

Lucian of Antioch: Martyr. Feast Day 7 January. 4th century priest, martyred under Diocletian. Drowned body brought ashore by dolphin.

Lucian of Beauvais: Martyr. Feast Day 8 January. 3rd century. Went from Rome as missionary to Gaul.

Lucy: Martyr. Feast Day 13 December. Martyred at Syracuse 304. Symbol, eyes on dish.

Ludmilla: Grandmother of St Wenceslas. 10th century — Bohemia.

Luke: Evangelist. Feast Day 18 October. 1st century. Patron saint of doctors and artists. Symbol, winged ox.

Malo: (Maclou): Missionary. Feast Day 15 November. Died Brittany c. 640.

Margaret (Marina) of Antioch: Feast Day 20 July. Early 4th century. Supposed to have been swallowed by devil disguised as dragon; made sign of cross and dragon burst open. Symbol, dragon.

Margaret of Scotland: Queen. Feast Day 16 November. 1045-1093. Cared for poor and orphans.

Marina: Feast Day 12 February. Lived in monastery as monk; kept her sex a secret even when accused of fathering illegitimate child; endured punishment. Sex and innocence discovered on her death.

Mark: Evangelist. Feast Day 25 April. 1st century. Symbol, winged lion.

Martha: Feast Day 29 July. 1st century. Sister of Mary and Lazarus. Supposed to have overcome dragon at Tarascon by sprinkling it with holy water.

Martin of Tours: Feast Day 11 November. Born Pannonia 315. Died near Tours 397. In art, dividing his cloak.

Martin de Porres: Born and died Lima, Peru, 1597-1639. Dominican laybrother. Cared for sick and destitute. In U.S. patron saint for those working for international understanding.

Lawrence O'Toole: Bishop. Feast Day 14 November. Born Leinster 1128. Died Eu, Normandy 1180. Archbishop of Dublin. Relics in church of St Laurent at Eu. Patron saint of Dublin.

Lazarus: 1st century. Feast Day 17 December. Brother of Mary and Martha. Raised from dead by Jesus. Undertook missionary journeys.

Leger: Martyr. Feast Day 2 October. Born 616. Died Arras 678. Bishop of

Autun, very strict. Had his eyes put out before being beheaded; is invoked against blindness.

Mary, Blessed Virgin: Principal Feast Day 15 August. Mother of Jesus.

Mary Magdalene: Feast day 22 July. 1st century. Anointed Jesus with precious ointment; present at crucifixion; first person to whom Jesus appeared after resurrection. Symbol, ointment jar. Supposed tomb at Aix-en-Provence, place of pilgrimage.

Matthew: Apostle, evangelist. Feast Day 21 September. 1st century. Symbol, angel.

Mattias: Apostle. Feast Day 24 February. Chosen to replace Judas. Symbol, axe.

Maudet (Mawes): 6 century.

Maurice (Moritz): Martyr. Feast Day 22 September. 3rd century. Christian soldier in Egyptian legion of Roman army. Refused to take part in sacrifice and put to death.

Méen: Abbot. Feast Day 21 June. 6th century. Established monastery of St Meen to which St Petroc's relics were taken for a short time.

Médard of Noyon: Bishop. Feast Day 8 June. 6th century. Various French sayings about St Médard weather similar to English ones about St Swithin.

Mellon: Bishop. Feast Day 22 October. Early 4th century. Born near Cardiff, settled in France. First bishop of Rouen.

Michael: Archangel. Feast Day 29 September. Sent to cast out Lucifer and weigh souls of the dead, so is portrayed with sword defeating dragon, or with scales.

Mildred: Abbess. Feast Day 13 July. C. 700. Educated at French convent. Entered convent founded by her mother at Minster, Thanet, and later became abbess.

Monica: Feast Day 4 May. Born Algeria 330. Died Ostia (near Rome) 387. Mother of St Augustine of Hippo.

Mungo: (See Kentigern).

Mylor: Martyr. Cornwall and Brittany. Had silver hand and brazen foot.

Neot: Monk. Feast Day 31 July.

Nicholas: Bishop. Feast Day 6 December. 4th century bishop of Myra. Symbol, three golden balls.

Nicholas von Flue: Feast Day 21 March. Born and died Switzerland, of which he is patron saint. 1417-1487. Decided to leave wife and ten children and live as hermit (with wife's consent).

Ninian: Missionary. Feast Day 16 September. 4th century.

Norbert: Bishop. Feast Day 6 June. Born Cologne 1080. Died Magdeburg

1134. Swallowed deadly spider in communion cup rather than spill consecrated wine; remained unharmed.

Odo: Abbot. Feast Day 18 November. Born and died Tours 879-942. Influential abbot of famous monastery at Cluny.

Olaf (Olave): King. Feast Day 29 July. Born and died Norway 995-1030.
Became king 1016; killed in battle with Danes. Regarded as national hero.

Oliver Plunket: Martyr. Born County Meath 1629. Died Tyburn.

Omer: Missionary. Feast Day 9 September. Born near Lake Constance. Died
670 in Pas-de-Calais where he founded abbey around which grew town of St
Omer. Blind for many years, is invoked against eye diseases.

Oswald of Northumbria: King. Feast Day 9 August. 605-642.

Oswald of Worcester: Bishop. Feast Day 28 February. 925-992. Born in England of Danish parents. Bishop of Worcester and archbishop of York. Established many monasteries, including Westbury-on-Trym, Ramsey
(Huntingdonshire), Evesham and Pershore.

Ottilia (Odilia): Abbess. Feast Day 13 December. Patron saint of Alsace.
Born blind so invoked against blindness. Cured at convent and became
deeply religious.

Ouen: Bishop. Feast Day 24 August. Born near Soissons 610. Died Clichy
687. Archbishop of Rouen. Founded monasteries, notably abbey at Rebaix.

Pancras: Martyr. Feast Day 12 May. Martyred in Rome c. 304 aged 14. St
Andrew's monastery built on land belonging to his family; when St
Augustine went from there to Kent, he dedicated church in Canterbury to St
Pancras, thus introducing name into England.

Pantaleon: Martyr. Feast Day 27 July. Early 4th century. Patron saint of doctors. Physician at court of Emperor Galerius.

Patrick: Patron saint of Ireland. Feast Day 17 March. Lived 385-461.

Paul: 'Apostle of the Gentiles'. Feast Day 29 June. Born Tarsus. Died Rome
c. 67.

Paul of Thebes: Hermit. Feast Day 15 January. Died 347 aged 100.

Paula: Feast Day 26 January. Born Rome 347. Died Bethlehem 404. Friend
of St Jerome.

Paulinus of York: Missionary. Feast Day 10 October. Born Rome. Died
Rochester 644.

Peter: Apostle. Feast Day 29 June. Died Rome c. 64.

Petroc: Abbot. Feast Day 4 June. 6th century.

Philip: Apostle. Feast Day 1 May. 1st century.

Philip Neri: Reformer. Feast Day 26 May. Born Florence 1515. Died Rome
1595. Formed group to help sick and pilgrims. Encouraged young to dance
and play games.

Phocas: Martyr. Feast Day 22 September. Market gardener at Sinope, near Black Sea. Entertained own executioners and dug his own grave.

Piran: Abbot. Feast Day 5 March. 6 century.

Pol de Leon: Bishop. Feast Day 12 March. 6th century. Went from Wales to Brittany and became bishop of St-Pol-de-Leon.

Polycarp: Martyr. Feast Day 23 February. Died Smyrna 155. Burned to death. Church at Smyrna wrote detailed account of his martyrdom and celebrated it annually at his tomb — first time a feast day was kept in this way.

Radegonde: Queen. Feast Day 13 August. Born Thuringia 518. Died Poitiers 587. Forced to marry Frankish King Clothaire. Left him and established Holy Cross convent at Poitiers. Patron saint of Jesus College, Cambridge.

Raphael: Archangel. Feast Day 29 September. Accompanied Tobias and provided ointment which healed his father's blindness. Symbol, jar of ointment.

Remi: Bishop. Feast Day 1 October. Born Laon 438. Died Rheims 533. Baptised King Clovis.

Richard of Chichester: Bishop. Feast Day 3 April. Born Droitwich 1197. Died Dover 1253. Bishop of Chichester 1244. Consecreted new church dedicated to St Edmund at Dover and died there.

Rita: Nun. Feast Day 22 May. Born Spoleto 1381. Died Cascia 1457. Miracles of doubtful authenticity as life not written for 150 years.

Robert de Molesme: Abbot. Feast Day 29 April. Born Troyes 1027. Died Molesme (Burgundy) 1111. Founder of Cistercians.

Roch (Rock, San Rocco): Healer. Feast Day 16 August. Born and died Montpellier. 14th century. Gave wealth to poor and went on pilgrimage to Rome. Nursed sick in plague-stricken towns. Stricken himself and kept alive by dog bringing him food. On return own family failed to recognise him and had him imprisoned as impostor. Truth revealed after his death. Invoked against disease. In art, with dog.

Rose of Lima: Feast Day 30 August. Born and died Lima, 1586-1671. First South American saint. Lived as recluse; had many mystical experiences.

Samson: Bishop. Feast Day 28 July. Born Wales c. 490. Died Dol, c. 565. Travelled Wales, Cornwall, Channel Islands and Brittany.

Scholastica: Twin sister of St Benedict. Born Nursia c. 480. Died near Monte Cassino 543.

Sebastian: Martyr. Feast Day 20 January. 3rd century. Symbol, arrow.

Serafina: Virgin. Feast Day 12 March. Born and died San Gimignano 1238-1253, aged 15. On day of death bells tolled on their own and wallflowers blossomed on walls of town.

Silas (Silvanus): Feast Day 13 July. 1st century. Worked with St Paul.

Simeon the Stylite: Feast Day 5 January. Born Cilicia 390. Died Telanissus 459.

Simon: Apostle. Feast Day 28 October. 1st century. Emblem, saw.

Sophia: Martyr. Feast Day 30 September. Legendary mother of Saints Faith, Hope and Charity. Church of St Sophia, Constantinople not dedicated to a saint; means Holy Wisdom and is dedicated to Christ as Word of God.

Stephen: First martyr. Feast Day 26 December. Emblem, stones.

Stephen (Etienne): Abbot. Feast Day 8 February. Lived 1046-1124. Founded community of hermit monks near Limoges. Canonised 1189 at request of Henry II of England.

Susanna: Martyr. Feast Day 11 August. 3rd century. Lived in Rome, niece of Pope Caius. Took vow of virginity and martyred together with her father.

Swithin (Swithun): Bishop. Feast Day 15 July. Died Winchester 862. At own request was buried with poor *outside* the cathedral. When clergy wanted to move body to tomb inside, heavy rain fell for 40 days making removal impossible.

Teilo: Bishop. Feast Day 9 February. 6th century. Born West Wales. Went on pilgrimage to Jerusalem with St David. Spent time in Brittany with St Samson. Founded monastery at Llandeilo. Venerated Wales and Brittany.

Teresa of Avila: Foundress, Doctor of the Church. Feast Day 15 October. 1515-1582. Mystical experiences; reformed Carmelite order.

Thecla: Martyr. Feast Day 23 September. 1st century. Betrothed to governor, but broke betrothal when she heard St Paul preaching; Paul imprisoned and Thecla arrested; survived fire and wild beasts; lived in cave like hermit; possessed healing powers.

Theodore: Martyr. Feast Day 9 November. 4th century. Roman soldier who refused to sacrifice. Set fire to temple of goddess Cybele. Overcame dragon in form of snake or crocodile. Soldier saint similar to St George.

Theodore of Canterbury: Feast Day 19 September. Born Tarsus 602. Died Canterbury 690.

Thomas: Apostle. Feast Day 21 December. 1st century. Symbol, carpenter's rule.

Thomas Aquinas: Theologian. Feast day 7 March. Born and died Italy 1225-1274. In art, shown in Dominican habit, holding book from which rays of light spread outwards. Symbol, star.

Thomas à Becket: Martyr. Feast Day 29 December. Born London 1118. Died Canterbury 1170. Archbishop of Canterbury, martyred in Cathedral.

Timothy: Martyr. Feast Day 24 January. 1st century; Lystra (Asia Minor). Converted by St Paul; became his friend and helper. Paul wrote two epistles to him. First bishop of Ephesus. Martyred for trying to stop heathen festival.

Ulrich: Bishop. Feast Day 4 July. Born Zurich 890. Died Augsberg 973. Bishop of Augsburg for 50 years. Canonised 993 by Pope John XV, first canonisation by papal decree.

Veronica: Feast Day 12 July. Compassionate woman who wiped Christ's face with a cloth on the way of Calvary. 'Veronica's veil' retained image preserved in St Peter's, Rome.

Vincent: Martyr. Feast Day 22 January. Died Valencia 304. Martyred under Diocletian. Patron saint of Lisbon.

Vincent de Paul: Founder. Feast Day 19 July. Born Pouay, (Landes) 1580. Died Paris 1660. Patron saint of charitable societies.

Vitus: Martyr. Feast Day 15 June. 4th century. Denounced as Christian, boiled in oil together with his old nurse. Emblem, cock.

Walburga: (Walpurgis): Abbess. Feast Day 25 February. Born Wessex. Died Germany 779. Nun at Wimborne, Dorset. Became head of double monastery at Heidenheim. Relics translated to Eichstatt. 'Walpurgis-nacht', 1st May associated with witchcraft. People flocked to shrine to see miraculous oil exuding from shrine.

Wenceslas: Duke of Bohemia. Feast Day 28 September 907-929. 'Good King Wenceslas' was only 22 when murdered. Converted by grandmother Ludmilla. Father killed when Wenceslas was still a child; pagan mother had Ludmilla killed and encouraged younger son, Boleslas, to murder Wenceslas. Patron saint of Czechoslovakia.

Werberga (Werburgh): Abbess. Feast Day 3 February. Died c. 700. English princess who became nun, founded several convents, died at Threckingham, Lincolnshire. Body later moved to Chester during Danish invasion.

Wilfrid: Bishop. Feast Day 12 October. 634-709. Born Northumbria. Educated Lindisfarne and Rome. Made bishop of Ripon and later bishop of York, displacing St Chad who went to Lichfield.

Wilgefortis (Uncumber): Feast Day 20 July. Legendary Portuguese princess. Patron saint of women with troublesome husbands.

Willebald: Bishop. Feast Day 7 July. Born Wessex c. 700. Died Eichstatt 786. Brother of St Walburga. First known English pilgrim to Holy Land; journey lasted six years. St Boniface made him first bishop of Eichstatt.

Willebrord: Bishop. Feast Day 7 November. Born Northumbria 658. Died Echternach 739. Educated at Ripon under St Wilfrid. Missionary to Friesland; archbishop of Utrecht; founded monastery at Echternach; preached in Denmark.

Winifred: Martyr. Feast Day 3 November. 7th century. Martyred at Holywell, North Wales.

Winwaloe: Abbot. Feast Day 3 March. 6th century. Honoured in Brittany and Cornwall.

Uncumber: (see Wilgefortis).

Ursula: Martyr. Feast Day 14 February. 4th century; Cologne.

Valentine: Martyr. Feast Day 14 February. 3rd century, Rome.

Yves (Ivo): Lawyer Priest. Feast Day 19 May. Born and died Brittany 1253-1303. Studied law at Paris and Orleans. Became judge, famous for fairness and honesty. Used legal knowledge to help poor. Patron saint of lawyers.

Zita: Domestic servant. Feast Day 27 April. Born and died Lucca 1218-1278. Became servant at 12 and remained in same house all her life. Ill-treated by hot-tempered master and lazy mistress and by other servants who disapproved of her hard work, but gradually won their respect. Did everything 'to please God'. Only left the house for church and to visit sick and poor. Patron saint of domestic servants. Emblem, bunch of keys.

Index

157